Sew Pretty
for Little Girls

Sew Pretty
for Little Girls

Over 20 simple
sewing projects in
timeless floral prints

Alice Caroline

D&C
David and Charles
www.stitchcraftcreate.co.uk

Contents

Introduction

This book is packed with totally straight-forward yet beautiful projects, with every step carefully explained. You'll find all the guidance you need to support you through the process, particularly if you are a newcomer to the wonderful world of sewing! I've heard many people say that they can't sew – it's not their thing – but if you have even a vague desire to have a go, there is still time, you can learn. Sometimes past or school experiences can be off-putting, but the joy of trying as an adult is that no-one is there to grade you; you're free to enjoy the process and start at a level you feel comfortable with. You're doing it for you. You'll be surprised at how quickly your sewing skills build and how you can reconnect with your creativity to produce a project to be proud of. Or if you're already one of the converted, a confirmed sewing addict, I hope that the projects, fabrics and colour combinations in this book will provide fresh inspiration.

The projects in this book are arranged in three sections, but you can dive in wherever you like. The easiest projects are the Holly scatter cushions, the Gwen belt, the Fleur embellished party skirt and the Sara drawstring bag; all fun makes with beautiful, individual results.

There's nothing quite like the zen feeling of 'flow' that can come from working with your hands, doing a grounded task; the sensation of working with beautiful colours and textures; or the relaxation that comes from focusing on enjoyable work. Admittedly, it's not always like this – sometimes it can be so frustrating when you're unpicking what feels like miles of stitching! But there's a certain sense of triumph when you overcome a particular problem or keep persevering and it comes right in the end. I've also discovered a new awareness of what it takes to make something – an awareness that makes me appreciate the time and effort that's gone into making the shirt I'm wearing or the bedding I sleep in.

Make something special

Not so long ago clothes and fashion items were not as abundant as they are now. Nowadays so many things are readily available, that it makes it all the more special to make something individual. You have the choice of which colours and patterns to pair, so you can create something uniquely you.

Equally, bought gifts are lovely, but a unique handmade gift is a precious, appreciated thing indeed. Sometimes a project may be inspired by a friend: you might see a fabric and think 'ooh, she would love that', or perhaps the project item will be the starting point.

Seeing children playing with or wearing something that you made with your own hands can give you such a wonderful feeling of satisfaction. Your gift, whether it is a dress, a toy, a cushion or a quilt, becomes woven into their childhood. I love being able to create the same kinds of memories I've had for my kids, a new generation.

HAVE YOU EVER?:

❀ Wanted to express your creative side more, or rediscover it?

❀ Felt inspired to make something you know the tiny person in your life would love?

❀ Had the urge to create an heirloom that will be cherished and lovingly passed from mother to daughter?

❀ Wanted to play and experiment with colour and pattern but weren't sure where to start?

Hand-me-down skills

If your granny didn't teach you to sew, be not downhearted. There is an army of YouTube teachers out there, ready to give you all the tips and tricks you might need.

I was one of the lucky ones, coming to sewing through my grandma, and my mum. My grandma kept any clothing that was too worn to wear any more, and cut it up to use for the quilts she made. She hardly ever bought fabric because it was a dark era before quilting shops, and why would she when my grandfather's shirts did such a good job? My understanding of the importance and pleasure of making by hand came, foremost, from her because she was always quilting. It was a constant dawn-to-dusk activity that produced epic quilts, often given away as gifts. Not to mention the hand-crocheted tablecloth that took her 40 years to make, one tiny square a day. I must admit that although my grandmother did all of her quilting by hand, I prefer to use a machine for speed.

However, it was my mum who actually taught me to sew and took the time to teach me to patchwork, to cut out patterns and how to use a sewing machine. And it was my mum who inspired my love of bright colours. I then began to have an inkling of the satisfaction a creative life could bring.

After an eight-year adventure in scientific research, I rediscovered my 'maker' side, and started making bags, dresses and quilts, moving into designing patterns for bags and quilts, always with a mission to support new crafters through clear, detailed instructions. I have always admired Japanese sewing books, with step-by-step pictures that are so clear I'm able to follow the instructions without understanding a word of Japanese. Alongside designing, I started my business Alice Caroline, selling the patterns and an ever-growing curated range of Liberty Art Fabrics. I had always loved Liberty fabrics but they were hard to source, and I imagined that there must be others out there who shared my love.

WHERE DO YOU LIKE TO SEW?

❀ In your own crafting room or nook?

❀ On the kitchen table?

❀ Late at night after everyone has gone to bed?

❀ As a weekend project?

❀ With a group of friends, with family or a sewing group?

This sewing life

I tend towards the fly-by-night sewing – after the kids have gone to bed, and the house is quiet, I will head to my studio. It is also fun to attempt some simpler projects when the kids are around. They love being involved, and I like to think that even if they are just throwing fabric everywhere, they are beginning to learn a wonderful skill.

My sister laughs at my solution to the perennial 'I have nothing to wear' dilemma – I have been known to run up a dress the night before a wedding or party, on more than one occasion. Sometimes it's not quite finished on the inside but no one will know! I'm not saying I don't have a long-term, on-the-go project pile, but most appealing to me are the kind of simple projects I've shared with you in this book. I am always on the look-out for great projects that do not take up too much time – it's really satisfying to have beautiful results from one or two evening's work. The longer projects don't have to be done in one go – a couple of hours an evening will add up over a week or two.

Whatever your motivation, however you like to sew, using your own hands to produce something beautiful feels unbelievably good. You will be able to respond to 'wow, where did you get that from?' with a glowing 'I made it myself!'. I hope that you will love the process of making, and enjoy your finished treasures.

Fabrics

All of the fabrics you'll see in this book are from Liberty Art Fabrics, but all of these projects will be equally beautiful in other fabric lines – you don't necessarily have to stick with Liberty. Any fabric with a lightweight, dense weave and a bright, high-quality print will look absolutely gorgeous. However, you will need to bear in mind that at 137cm (54in) wide, Liberty fabrics are wider than regular printed cotton fabrics, which tend to be 121cm (44in) wide. For a bright and pretty look:

❀ Choose a patterned fabric, perhaps with a floral print, that has a small repeat – so that you see a good amount of the pattern, even on the smallest of skirts.

❀ Try to find cotton fabric with a high-thread count – you can tell by how soft and silky it feels to the touch. However, any kind of fabric will work with most of these projects.

❀ Don't be afraid to combine a variety of different prints – a good way to start is to choose your absolute favourite, then use the colours in it to pick out other co-ordinating fabrics.

Tip
You could mix in vintage floral fabrics, perhaps from old dresses that you no longer wear.

I love working with Liberty Tana Lawn, it is 100 per cent high-thread-count cotton but often feels almost silk-like, yet it 'behaves' so well with a sewing machine! It is very easy to sew with and so versatile. The quality of the print enables a very detailed design – miniature florals in high definition.

Liberty fabrics are instantly recognizable and have a timeless quality – the classics never seem to date, even though some of the fabrics still 'in print' are designs that are over 100 years old. Liberty regularly update these classics in contemporary colourways. Seasonal collections are designed by the in-house Art Fabrics team and they take inspiration from a range of situations and themes, often collaborating with well-known artists. Many of the collections are designed by referencing Liberty's extraordinary archive. I especially admire the creativity and artistry behind the prints.

One of the favourite parts of my job is receiving the new-season swatch book from Liberty, and searching through it for my favourite classic prints in gorgeous new colourways, or inventive new-season designs, to order for my shop. Part of the Liberty appeal is its heritage: my customers often get in touch and reminisce, about their childhood memories of the fabric, their first Liberty dress and first visit to the Liberty of London store, an emporium of wonder.

For plain fabrics I like to use Oakshott fabrics as they are high-quality cotton and come in a rainbow range of colours, some plain and some shot – where the warp and weft threads are different colours giving a beautiful iridescent look to the fabric.

I keep every single scrap of fabric, even tiny ones, you never know when they'll come in handy for a sewing or craft project, or perhaps inspire a mini patchwork project, such as one of the Orla pencil cases in this book.

Beautiful detailed prints in a rainbow of colours are just right for little girls' clothes and homewares. I hope the following projects inspire you!

Colour

I think my love of playing with colour began at school when I was supposed to be doing homework but instead fiddled around with the pencil crayons that had fallen out of their tin in my bag, rearranging them back into the rainbow (perhaps disagreeing with the order printed on the box!).

Then, when I started out playing with fabrics, it was mostly rainbows. My anatomy of a rainbow starts with red and goes through pink, orange, yellow, green, turquoise, to blue then purple. Sometimes maybe pink comes first. If I'm going to loop the rainbow back round again, I'll go from purple to pink then red and through the rainbow again. I break this down further into grading from light to dark within a shade so, for example, light pink comes first, then medium followed by dark pink. Also, I note the variations within a shade: amongst the greens there may be lime green, leaf green and blue-greens – the lime green would go next to the yellows, the leaf in the middle and the blue-greens and teals next to the turquoises or

blues. Within the purples, violet would come first, then brighter purples and plums followed by deep indigos. If brown and black were to feature they would go after purple in that order.

Another way I'll arrange colours, particularly for a quilt, is to start with a fabric I like most, usually a slightly larger scale print. I'll pick out the colours from it and find a fabric in each of those colours. When you're not sure where to begin when choosing fabrics for a project, a good starting point is to just pick your favourite fabric and match other fabrics around its colour theme. Another handy place to start is to use fabrics from a particular collection: the fabric designer has already co-ordinated the colour theme for you. Or perhaps branch out and add your own selection of fabrics into the mix.

Colour confidence

A great way to build your confidence is by being inspired by other people's colour combinations, just until you're ready to branch out on your own. You can learn what feels right to you by perhaps at first borrowing colour combinations and, when you feel drawn to change the order, that's the place where you can start to find your 'thing' or 'look'. My colour sense may not appeal to everyone, but I now have a sense of what works and doesn't work for me. When I used to try to think about what other people would like, it would all go horribly wrong, and no-one would be interested. I finally learnt to have the confidence to say: 'If I like it – I'll just do it'.

I'm on a mission to encourage people who think they are rubbish with colour to mess around, to play, to start again when things go wrong, to just

keep going. I've never used a colour wheel – I have to admit, I don't get them! – so don't worry if they don't work for you. On the other hand, you might find one handy. Anything goes.

Inspired by colour

One of the ways I play around with colour is simple but effective: the big inspiration board behind my desk, where I pin interesting or colourful items that come my way. Postcards, my most-loved family photos and holiday pictures, pages from magazines, beautiful business cards, scraps of fabric – it's a great way to see themes emerge and let exciting colour combinations arise through random pairings of images.

I also love using the virtual pinboard, Pinterest, and I try to blog whenever I've made something I'm excited to share. I find it invaluable and inspiring to see how fabrics come alive when you see them in use. Sometimes a piece of fabric that you initially may not have given a second look takes on a whole new appeal when you see it as a dress or together with other fabrics in a quilt. I hope the blog gets people excited about the possibilities of making their own individual clothes and homewares, and encourages those who aren't sure where to start.

Don't be afraid to experiment!

I don't think anyone is born with a style or that being great with colour just comes naturally. It's something that is developed through playing, through continually putting things together, mixing them up and changing them around, and through trusting your instincts (or working until you find them again!). You may not know why you like drawn to a particular colour or print, you might find yourself drawn to something you wouldn't normally go for, give it a chance, go with it… see where it leads. That's the way to learn and develop your own sensibility.

We all put colours together every day in the clothes we wear. By paying attention to what we love, and feeling free to experiment and try again if something doesn't work, we can gradually come to an awareness of our own unique colour sense and have true confidence in our creations.

Equipment

Pins
Glass-headed pins are easy to pick up and won't melt if ironed over!

Measuring tape
A flexible measuring tape is indispensable. Mine has inches and centimetres on the same side.

Pencil
I use a regular pencil for transferring markings and tracing patterns. If working with darker fabrics, a white pencil makes a stronger colour marking, particularly a washable watercolour pencil.

Scissors
I use Fiskars 21cm (9in) dressmaking scissors exclusively for cutting fabric, and another pair for cutting paper and everything else. I also use a small pair of Ernest Wright fine craft scissors for trimming threads and clipping seams. I highly recommend a scissor sharpener too!

Seam ripper
Very handy! Take care not to catch the fabric – as Liberty fabric is fine it is very easy to do.

Iron and ironing board
I very rarely use an iron for clothes, but I do absolutely use an iron to press when sewing. It's essential for a neat finish and preventing puckering problems at seams.

Hand sewing needles
I use sharps for most types of sewing.

Thimble
Use for sewing the skirt on Mia doll.

Rotary cutter, grid ruler and self-heal mat
Not essential but very useful, particularly for quilt making (makes cutting squares and strips super easy!). Use a 36 x 24in (90 x 60cm) mat and 24½ x 6½in (62 x 16cm) grid ruler. The ruler also shows a 45-degree angle – handy when marking a diamond grid for quilting.

Craft knife
I use a Stanley knife or Swann Morton scalpel and change the blades regularly.

Sewing machine
A basic model is all you need: keep your handbook safe and refer to it for essentials, such as altering the stitch length and how to make your machine do zigzag stitching.

Sewing Sundries

D-rings
I've used these for the Gwen belt. They are perfect for a child's belt as they adjust for a perfect fit, even as the child grows.

Popper tape
Just a bit easier than sewing on individual poppers, you do need to make sure that you have aligned one half of the tape accurately with the other so that the poppers meet, for example at the closure of the Lilly duvet cover.

Washable glue stick
I find a glue stick really handy for holding fabric in place temporarily before appliqué (particularly when I don't want to use a fusible interfacing/webbing). I use Coccoina as it is solvent free, washable and doesn't stain.

Fusible interfacing and fusible webbing
An interfacing is used when the project requires stiffness, like the Isabel baskets. The brand Vilene makes many different kinds of iron on (fusible) or sew in, all in different weights. (I used Vilene's Decovil 1 Light, which is a firm interfacing, for the base of the Isabel baskets.) Vilene also make Bondaweb, a lightweight fusible webbing that is like a permanent 'double-sided' sticky tape but for fabric. You fuse it to one fabric (with heat/iron) then peel off the backing paper and fuse it to another fabric, and it is perfect for appliqué.

Thread
For quilting, piecing fabrics together and quilt stitches I usually use one cream colour thread for everything: Colour 169 by Gutterman, either 100 per cent polyester or 100 per cent cotton. For other projects I will match the thread colour to the fabric. It's nice to build up a rainbow collection of threads over time.

Stuffing
I used 100 per cent polyester, which is machine washable and hypo-allergenic. Natural wool stuffing is also a good choice.

Buttonhole elastic
Ideal when making an easily adjustable waistband.

Quilt wadding (batting)
There are many kinds of wadding (batting) available. I use 100 per cent cotton as it is soft, natural and hypo-allergenic.

Blissful Bedrooms

What little girl wouldn't love a bedroom as colourful as this? All of these projects together create an amazing effect, but even just one cushion or doll's quilt will add magic to any space and make a treasured gift.

Cushions are a great place to start, as they are so easy to whip up. Even the quilt is less complex than you may think – it grows quickly and only requires you to be able to sew in a straight line. Colour-wise, you could go the rainbow route, choose contrasting tones or a cool graded look. Have fun experimenting to get the effect you want.

Sophie Quilt

This quilt is the largest project you'll find in this book – but don't let that put you off. Whether you are a seasoned quilter or yet to dip your toe in the water, this is a beautiful, fun and above all easy project to make.

This single bed-size quilt has many uses – it can be a cape, a tent a landscape, the possibilities are endless. Then again, it could just be something to snuggle up in while sharing your favourite story. You'll be sewing a timeless, evocative heirloom to be treasured forever.

You need 12 of your favourite pink and blue fabrics. By adding some pretty backing fabric this quilt becomes reversible, too!

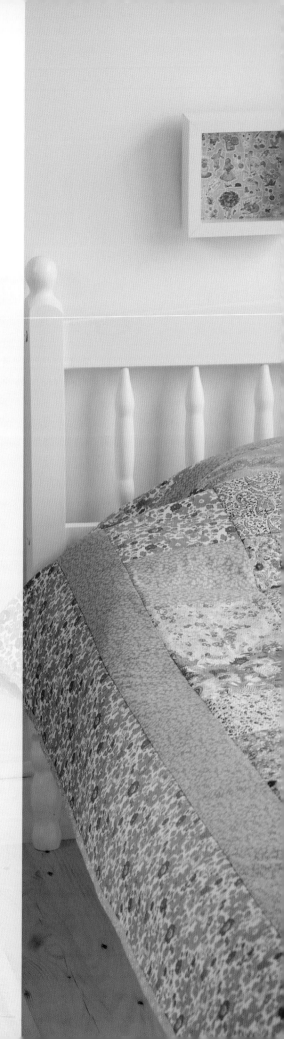

You will need

For a 137 x 229cm (54 x 90in) quilt

Wadding (batting): single quilt size or
150 x 240cm (58 x 94in)

If using 137cm (54in) wide Liberty fabric

Patchwork squares: a fat quarter, 0.25m (¼yd),
of each of 12 different fabrics

Backing fabric: 3m (3¼yd)

Inner border fabric: 0.5m (½yd)

Outer border fabric: 1m (1yd)

Binding fabric: 0.25m (¼yd), or 8m (9yd) of
ready-made 1.5cm (⅝in) or 2cm (¾in) wide bias
binding

If using regular 121cm (44in) wide fabric

Patchwork squares: a fat quarter, 0.25m (¼yd),
of each of 12 different fabrics

Backing fabric: 4.5m (5yd)

Inner border fabric: 0.75m (¾yd)

Outer border fabric: 1.25m (1½yd)

Binding fabric: 0.32m (⅓yd), or 8m (9yd) of
ready-made 1.5cm (⅝in) or 2cm (¾in) wide bias
binding

Cutting

- Cut six 15.5cm (6½in) squares of each of your
  12 fabrics to give 72 squares in total.
- Cut the backing fabric: if using Liberty fabric,
  cut in half to make two pieces 1.5m (59in); if
  using regular fabric, cut into three pieces, each
  approximately 1.5m (59in).
- Inner border: cut across the width (from
  selvedge to selvedge) into 9cm (3½in) strips.
- Outer border: cut across the width (from
  selvedge to selvedge) into 15.5cm (6½in) strips.
- Binding: cut into 4cm (1½in) strips (this is not
  necessary if using ready-made bias binding).

FABRIC COLOUR NOTES

I chose predominantly pink and turquoise
fabrics, adding a further couple of fabrics that
included these colour plus more colours, such
as yellow, green and slightly darker blue. I used
four turquoise, six pink and two multicoloured
prints. Or you could start by choosing your
favourite multicoloured fabric and pick another
11 fabrics based on the colours in that fabric.

Tip

If the bed you are making the quilt for has a foot board, you may wish to make a shorter quilt. Leave out 12 squares, that is to say one of the blocks described in step 5, below. This will give a finished quilt size of 137 x 198cm (54 x 78in).

All seam allowances are 5mm (¼in) unless otherwise stated.

Piecing

1 With right sides together, sew two squares of different fabric together down one edge.

Tip

For speed, use the chain piecing method described in the Techniques section.

2 Open out and press the seam to one side, pressing it towards the darkest fabric. Repeat steps 1 and 2 with all the remaining squares, until you have all 36 sets of squares sewn together.

3 With right sides together, sew two pairs of squares together. Make sure that you always sew two different fabrics together to create a good mix.

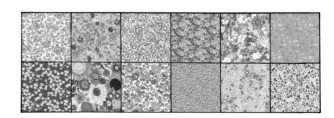

4 Open out and press the seam to one side. Repeat with all remaining pairs from step 2. Now you will have 18 sets of four squares joined together. Again, you should aim to have four different fabrics per block.

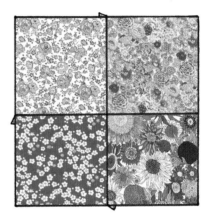

5 Place a block of four squares on top of another block of four squares, with right sides together, and sew down one edge to make a block of eight squares. Open out and press the seam to one side. Place another block of four squares on top of the four you have just added, with right sides together, and align the short edge. Sew along the short edge. Open out to give a block of two by six squares. Press the seam to one side. Repeat with remaining blocks of four squares. You will now have six lots of blocks of two by six squares.

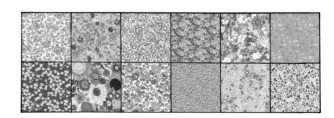

6 Lay out your six blocks on the floor and arrange as well as you can to achieve a fairly random distribution of different fabrics. Try to avoid having two of the same fabrics next to each other.

Tip

Take a photograph, or label each block 1, 2, 3 etc, to help you remember the order before you sew the blocks together.

7 Take one block of two by six squares and place another on top with right sides together. Sew together along the long edge. Open out and press the seam to one side. Sew the next block from step 5 to this new block.

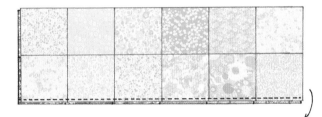

8 Repeat step 7 until all the blocks from step 5 have been sewn together giving you a quilt top of six by 12 squares.

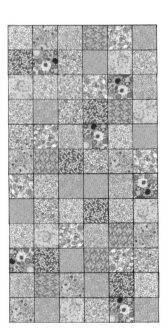

9 Next prepare the inner border. Sew your 9cm (3½in) strips together, short end to short end, placing them right sides together one at a time, to make one very long strip. From this long strip cut off two strips each 120cm (47in) long and two strips each 193cm (76in) long.

10 Lay one of the 193cm (76in) strips on top of your quilt top, right sides together, aligning the long edges and allowing the border to overhang the quilt by about 5cm (2in) at either end. Stitch together. Repeat with the other long inner border strip on the opposite side of the quilt.

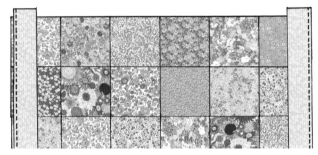

Sophie Cot Quilt

This project can be scaled down to make a cot quilt measuring 91.5 x 122cm (36 x 48in). Take 12 different fabrics – you need a 33cm (13in) square of each. Cut four 15.5cm (6½in) squares each to give you a total of 48 squares. Sew them together to give a finished quilt top of six by eight squares. Don't add a border, just continue from the Layer and Quilt instructions for the Sophie quilt. You'll need a backing fabric cut to 101.5 x 132cm (40 x 52in) and 4.75m (5yd) of binding.

11 Trim the excess length of border fabric level with the top of the quilt. Open out the border and press the seams to one side. Then trim the excess at bottom of the quilt in the same way.

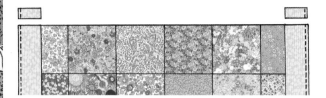

12 To add the inner border to the top and bottom edges, lay one of your 120cm (47in) strips on top of the quilt, with right sides together, aligning the top edges and stitch together. Repeat at the bottom of quilt. Open out, press the seams to one side. Trim as you did in step 11.

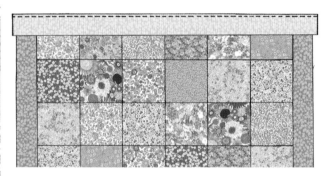

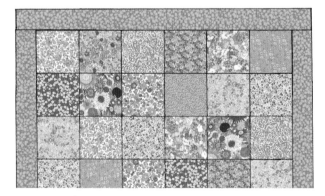

13 Next prepare the outer border. Sew your 15.5cm (6½in) strips, with right sides together, end to end (short ends together) to make one very long strip. From this long strip, cut off two 152.5cm (60in) long strips and two 211cm (83in) long strips.

14 To add the outer border, lay one of the 211cm (83in) strips on top of your quilt, right sides together, aligning the long edges and allowing the border to overhang the quilt by about 5cm (2in) at either end. Stitch together. Repeat with the other long border at the opposite side of the quilt. Open out and press the seam to one side. Trim as in step 11.

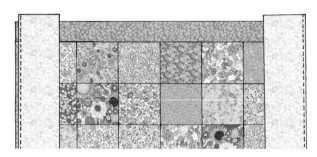

15 Next lay one of your 152.5cm (60in) outer border strips on top of your quilt, with right sides together, aligning the edges and stitch together. Repeat at the bottom of the quilt. Open out and press the seams to one side, trim as you did in step 11.

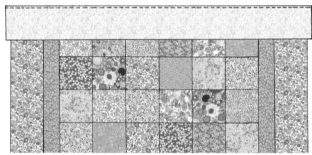

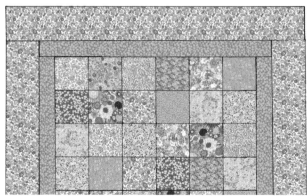

16 Now prepare your quilt backing by joining your backing fabric pieces together. If you are using regular fabric, take two pieces of the backing fabric and place one on top of the other, right sides together, and stitch together along the selvedges (the longest edge). Open out and add the third piece, right sides facing and stitch along the selvedges to make one large piece. Open the seams and press. Trim so that your backing piece measures 150 x 240cm (58 x 94in). If you are using Liberty fabric, stitch your two pieces of backing fabric together, right sides together, along the selvedge using a 1cm (3⁄8in) seam. Press the seam open. Trim so your backing piece measures 150 x 240cm (58 x 94in).

Layer and Quilt

1 Place your quilt backing, right side down, on a flat surface. Place the wadding (batting) on top, smoothing out any bumps, and place your pieced quilt top on top, right side up.

Tip
Pull the edges of the quilt backing gently at opposite sides to remove any wrinkles.

2 Smooth all over the top of the quilt with your hands to ensure all layers are flat. Tack (baste) the layers together – see Hand Sewing Stitches: Running Stitch in Techniques (you will remove these stitches later). Alternatively, use washable adhesive to stick the layers together, or pin them together with safety pins (place one pin in the centre of each square and every 15cm (6in) or so along the borders).

3 Stitch whatever pattern you like all over the top of the quilt. I kept it simple and stitched 'in the ditch', which means along the seams between the patchwork squares.

Tip
Start sewing in the centre of the quilt and work out towards the edges to reduce puckering.

Bind the Edges

1. Trim the edges of all the layers of the quilt so they are straight and the corners are right angles.

2. Prepare the binding. If you are using ready-made bias binding, just open out one side and press. If you are making your own binding, sew your 4cm (1½in) strips together, end to end (short ends together), to make one really long strip. Fold over 5mm (¼in) all along one long edge and press. Cut the binding into four pieces: two 150cm (58in) long and two 240cm (94in) long.

3. Take one piece of 240cm (94in) long binding and align it with one of the longer edges of the reverse of the quilt, with right sides together. Sew the binding to the reverse of the quilt, stitching through all the quilt layers, 5mm (¼in) from the edge.

4. Fold the binding around the raw edge of the quilt to the front of the quilt.

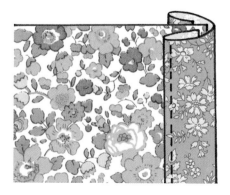

5. Turn the quilt over and, ensuring that the binding covers up the stitches from step 3, topstitch the folded edge of the binding to the quilt top, stitching through all the layers. (On the back of the quilt, your stitches should lie next to the binding.) Trim the ends of the binding level with the top and bottom quilt edges. Repeat steps 3 to 5 for the other long side of the quilt.

6. Repeat step 3 along the top edge of the quilt using one of the 150cm (58in) strips of binding and leaving an excess of about 2.5cm (1in) at the beginning and end of the quilt edge. Trim this binding overhang to 1cm (³/₈in) beyond the quilt edge at both ends.

7. Bring the overhanging end of the binding round the edge of the quilt to the front, then fold the rest of the binding strip over the top edge of the quilt and topstitch (as you did in step 5). Repeat to finish off the overhang of the binding at the other end.

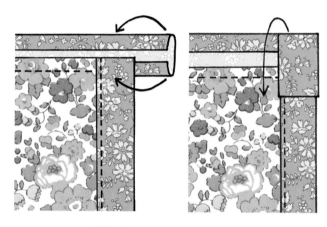

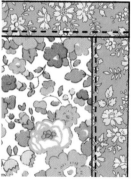

8. Repeat steps 6 and 7 at the bottom edge of the quilt. Your quilt is now finished!

Annie Doll Quilt

This doll quilt is just waiting to wrap up a favourite doll – the Mia doll would certainly be happy with such a lovely coverlet! Its cute patchwork surface can double as a playmat for a teddy bears' tea party, and it's lovely on the reverse too. I chose fabrics with a storybook theme, in this case Alice in Wonderland, for extra playtime fun.

Holly Scatter Cushions

A colourful nest of cushions makes any spot feel warm and inviting, whether it's a sumptuous corner armchair or a big comfy bed.

You can use this straightforward set of instructions to make a variety of cushions, some plain and some appliquéd, and in three different sizes. With an envelope-style back, these cushions don't involve any fiddly zips or buttons, so you really can make lots, with time left over to sink back into them and share a story or two.

Choose your colours to match the bedroom's theme, or co-ordinate with your gorgeous homemade Sophie Quilt!

You will need

For a 30cm (12in) square cushion

Cut fabric size 33 x 73.5m (13 x 29in)

For a 40cm (16in) square cushion

Cut fabric size 43 x 96.5cm (17 x 38in)

For a 46cm (18in) square cushion

Cut fabric size 48 x 109cm (19 x 43in)

FABRIC COLOUR NOTES

Choose fabrics to go with the theme of the room or pick out colours from the Sophie quilt. I sometimes make these cushions as presents, the colours and prints being inspired by the recipient!

Making

1 Select your fabric and cut to the right size for the cushion that you would like to make.

2 At one end of the short edge of the fabric, fold over 5mm (¼in) to the wrong side and press.

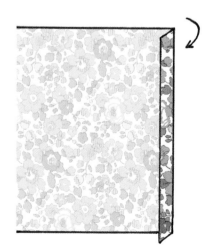

3 Fold over another 1cm (½in) and press. Topstitch through all the layers, making sure to stay close to the edge of the original fold.

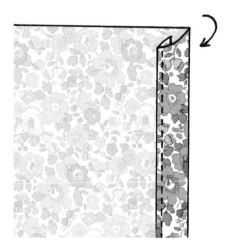

4 Repeat steps 1 to 3 at the other end of the fabric.

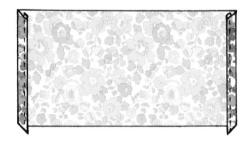

5 Lay the fabric out with the right side facing up and fold one end of the fabric over on top. This measurement is 19cm (7½in) for the 30cm (12in) cushion, 25cm (10in) for the 40cm (16in) cushion and 30cm (11½in) for the 46cm (18in) cushion.

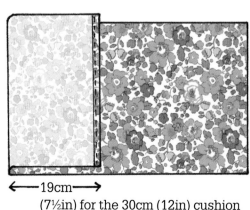

←——19cm——→
(7½in) for the 30cm (12in) cushion

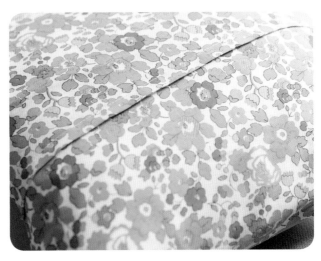

6 Fold over the other end of the fabric by about the same amount as in step 5 and, most importantly, ensure the bottom layer is as wide as the finished size of your cushion: 30cm (12in) wide for the 30cm (12in) square cushion, 40cm (16in) wide for the 40cm (16in) square cushion and 46cm (18in) wide for the 46cm (18in) square cushion.

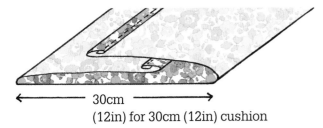

← 30cm →
(12in) for 30cm (12in) cushion

7 Stitch through all layers, 1cm (½in) from the raw edges, down each side of the folded fabric leaving the overlapped edges open for an envelope-style back.

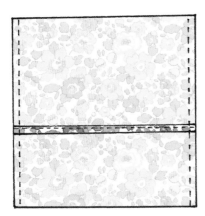

8 Turn the finished cushion cover right side out through the back opening. Press and insert the cushion pad.

Rosie Floor Cushion

Little girls will love this patchwork floor cushion, whether for lounging on or jumping on! Having several scattered around not only looks beautiful but also creates the perfect venue for story time or playing with friends.

The rainbow colours of this floor cushion make me so happy and the 'log cabin' patchwork pattern is perfect for using smaller strips of your favourite fabrics. You'll find that the strip piecing method is an easy one to master, and produces a really satisfying look that is a lovely mix of classic and contemporary design.

You will need

For a 69cm (27in) square cushion

One 9cm (3½in) square of fabric (A)

6.5cm (2½in) wide strips of 12 different fabrics (B–M)

Backing fabric, 70cm (27½in) square

Cushion pad, 69cm (27in) square

FABRIC COLOUR NOTES

I wanted to create an obvious rainbow effect for this cushion, so I chose a whole spectrum of colours and arranged them as follows, from left to right: dark purple, medium purple, pale purple/violet, dark blue, medium blue, turquoise/light blue, turquoise, green, yellow, pale pink, medium pink, medium/dark pink, dark pink/red.

Cutting

- Cut the 6.5cm (2½in) strips as follows:
- Bi: 9cm (3½in), Bii: 14cm (5½in), Ci: 14cm (5½in), Cii: 19cm (7½in), Di: 19cm (7½in), Dii: 24cm (9½in), Ei: 24cm (9½in), Eii: 29cm (11½in), Fi: 29cm (11½in), Fii: 34cm (13½in), Gi: 34cm (13½in), Gii: 39cm (15½in), Hi: 39cm (15½in), Hii: 44cm (17½in), Ii: 44cm (17½in), Iii: 49cm (19½in), Ji: 49cm (19½in), Jii: 54cm (21½in), Ki: 54cm (21½in), Kii: 59cm (23½in), Li: 59cm (23½in), Lii: 64cm (25½in), Mi: 64cm (25½in), Mii: 69cm (27½in).

All seam allowances are 5mm (¼in) unless otherwise stated.

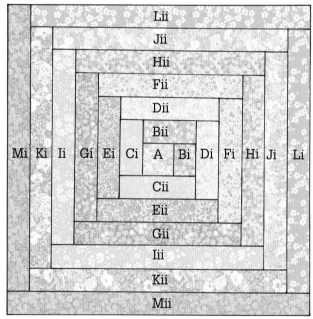

Tip

If you find it difficult to locate a 69cm (27in) square cushion pad, substitute it for a standard 66cm (26in) cushion pad (for a loose fit) or a standard 72cm (28in) square cushion pad if you prefer a tighter fit.

Piecing

1 Take square A and place strip Bi, right sides together, on top. Sew together along the right-hand edge.

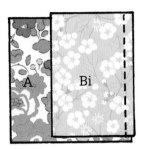

2 Open out and press the seam to one side, away from the centre square.

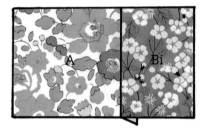

3 Sew strip Bii to the unit you made in step 1, across the top of A and Bi. Open out and press the seam to one side, away from the centre.

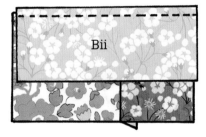

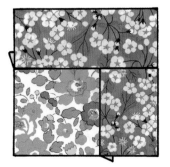

4 Sew strip Ci to the piece you made in step 3, joining it across the edges of A and Bii. Open out and press the seam away from the centre as before.

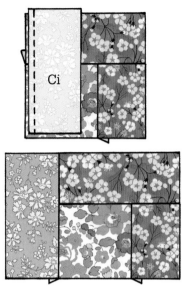

5 Next add strip Cii, and continue adding strips in this way in alphabetical order: Di, Dii, Ei, Eii, Fi, Fii etc. Mii is the last strip, which completes the log cabin top of the cushion.

6 Lay your backing fabric right side up on a flat surface. Place your cushion top, right sides together, on top of your backing fabric. Sew all around the edges, leaving a 50cm (20in) gap down one side. Stitch around the edges again to create a strong seam (leaving the gap again). Turn right side out and press.

7 Insert the cushion pad and close the gap with slip stitch or ladder stitch (see Hand Sewing Stitches in the Techniques section).

Lilly Duvet and Pillow Set

Whatever your level of sewing experience, you can create this bright and snuggly focus for a bedroom. The lucky little girl you're making this for will drift off to sleep wrapped up in super-soft cotton. Reversible, long-lasting, versatile and, if you choose, covered in flying merry-go-round carnival ponies! This will be a big hit.

I have to share with you an amazing invention that I have discovered – popper tape. This means that there is no fiddly sewing-on of individual poppers or buttons, making this bedding set a much speedier job than you might think. Enjoy!

You will need

For a standard single duvet and pillow

2.5m (2¾yd) each of two co-ordinating fabrics at least 137cm (54in) wide (Liberty or sheeting fabric)

86cm (34in) popper tape or eight poppers

FABRIC COLOUR NOTES

I chose two different fabrics here with the same theme – pink ponies! The print on one is densely patterned with lots of similar sized ponies, so at a distance it is more intensely coloured. The other fabric follows the same theme but with a more expanded print. It features larger and more varying sized ponies, in the same colourway, but the bigger motifs have more space between them on a white background, giving the design an overall less intense colour.

Tip

You can make a 40cm (16in) cushion cover with the two leftover pieces of fabric. Stitch them together (right sides together) along one edge with a 1cm (⅜in) seam and follow the instructions for the Holly scatter cushions.

Cutting

- Duvet cover: cut 2m (2¼yd) of full width of both fabrics, leave selvedges on.
- Pillowcase: cut 92 x 50cm (36 x 21in) of the fabric for the top of the pillow, and 78 x 50cm (30½ x 21in) of your other fabric.

All seam allowances are 1cm (⅜in) unless otherwise stated.

Making

For the duvet cover

1 Begin by making a hem on one short edge of one 2m (2¼yd) piece of fabric. Fold up 1cm (⅜in) of fabric to the wrong side and press. Fold up another 4cm (1½in) and press. Stitch close to the fold through all the layers and press again. Repeat with the other 2m (2¼yd) fabric piece.

2 Un-pop the two halves of the popper tape, then machine zigzag stitch to finish the ends of the tape neatly. With the fabric for the duvet cover right side up, centre one of the halves of the popper tape across the width of the duvet cover along bottom edge, within the hem, and pin. Stitch around all the edges of the popper tape to secure it. Alternatively, apply individual poppers according to the manufacturer's instructions.

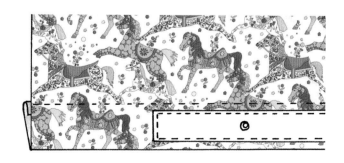

3 Repeat step 2 with the other 2m (2¼yd) fabric piece and the other half of the popper tape. Make sure that the poppers align with their other halves on the opposite side of the duvet cover.

5 Starting from one edge, stitch across the bottom of the duvet cover, just above the hem to 1cm (⅜in) past the start of the popper tape. Then stitch across the end of the tape to the bottom of the duvet cover.

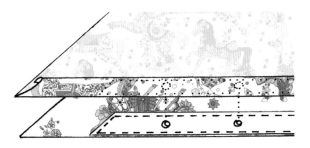

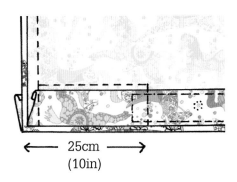

25cm (10in)

4 Lay one duvet cover piece on top of the other, right sides together. Pin all around the edges. Starting at one bottom corner, stitch the layers together all along one long edge, across the top and down the other side. Finish the seam (see Techniques section).

6 Turn right side out and press the seams. Your duvet cover is complete; slip it over your duvet and popper it up.

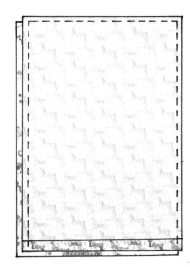

Tip

If you're not using popper tape, apply individual poppers about every 13cm (5in), remembering to align the poppers with their other halves on the opposite side of the duvet cover.

For the pillowcase

1 Take the pillowcase top fabric piece and with the wrong side facing up, at the right-hand end, fold 1cm (⅜in) over, press, then fold over another 1cm (⅜in) and press again. Make a line of stitching, close to this fold, through all the layers.

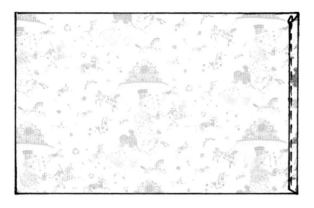

Tip

Calling the fabric pieces 'top' and 'bottom' is only really relevant if you are using different patterned fabrics and want one to be the one that ends up on top.

2 Take the bottom pillowcase fabric piece and with the wrong side facing up, at the left-hand end, fold 1cm (⅜in) over, press, then fold another 5cm (2in) over, and press again. Stitch through all the layers close to the fold.

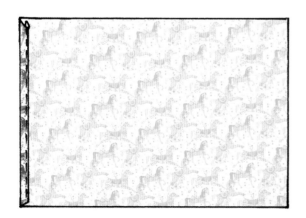

3 Place the top pillowcase piece right side up on a flat surface, folded edge at the left. Place the bottom pillow piece, folded edge also at the left, right side down on top. Align the right-hand edges. Fold about 18cm (7in) of your top pillowcase piece over on top of the bottom piece, and pin the edges together. Stitch through all the layers, around three sides but not along the folded edge.

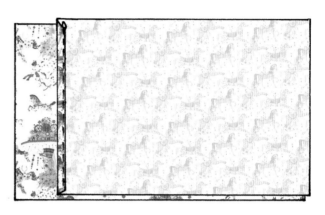

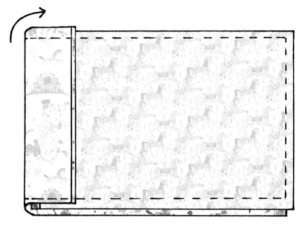

4 Finish the seam (see the Techniques section). Turn the right side out and press. Slip your pillow inside the finished pillowcase.

Lilly Duvet and Pillow Set

Natasha Tab Top Curtains

Bright and beautiful curtains instantly lift a room. These ones use raw edge appliqué to make a kaleidoscope of butterflies flutter through your little one's window. How great is it that 'kaleidoscope' is one of the collective nouns for butterflies?

You can make your curtains sheer and breezy, with a blind behind, or line them for a more cosy look. The tab top means they'll sit flat when closed to show off your handiwork to the maximum, and is straightforward to create.

You will need

For curtains adapted to fit

Tab fabric: each tab requires 13 x 23cm (5 x 9in), so you will get five tabs out of 13cm (5in) of a 114cm (45in) wide fabric. For a 127cm (50in) wide curtain you will need two strips of fabric 13 x 114cm (5 x 45in) as tabs are spaced at intervals of approximately 13cm (5in) across the top width of the curtain

Curtain fabric: measure the width of your window and multiply by 1.5, next measure the height of your window, and add the distance of the drop below the windowsill you would like the curtain to be, plus the height above the window, plus 5cm (2in) for seam allowances

Additional strip of curtain fabric: to measure the width of your curtain x 10cm (4in)

Appliqué fabric: I used 14 different coloured fabrics for butterflies and enough to make 50 butterflies for a curtain measuring 127cm (50in) wide and 110cm (44in) high

Lightweight fusible webbing, enough for all of your butterflies

FABRIC COLOUR NOTES

For these curtains, I chose a white background in a lightweight cotton (Tana Lawn) that is almost sheer when hung against a window. I used 14 different colours for the butterflies in a rainbow of colours: dark purple, medium purple, pale purple/violet, dark blue, medium blue, turquoise/light blue, turquoise, green, yellow, pale pink, medium pink, medium/dark pink, dark pink/red.

All seam allowances are 1cm (⅜in) unless otherwise stated.

Making

1 Prepare all your butterflies first: fuse the lightweight fusible webbing to the wrong side of the appliqué fabrics, and cut the butterfly shapes out using the templates (see Templates). Remove the paper backing from the fusible webbing.

2 Spread the curtain fabric out on a flat surface. (I laid mine out on a towel on the floor, so I could iron the butterflies on without moving it to the ironing board!) Place the butterflies on the curtain, unbacked side facing up, and when you are happy with their position, pin in position then fuse in place. I chose to have my butterflies all facing at one angle, with the rainbow of colours red through to purple from top to bottom.

3 If you choose to, sew close to the edge around the butterflies using co-ordinating thread to complete the raw edge appliqué. However, this will take quite some time so, as the fused butterflies are secure, you can omit this step if you wish.

4 To prepare the curtain tabs, take a 13 x 114cm (5 x 45in) strip and fold it in half lengthwise with right sides together. Stitch along the long edge with a 5mm (¼in) seam to make a tube as shown. Turn right side out (see instructions in the Techniques section), and press the tube flat with the seam running in the centre of one flat side. Cut the flattened tube into five 13cm (5in) long curtain tabs. Repeat until you have all the tabs you need for your curtain width.

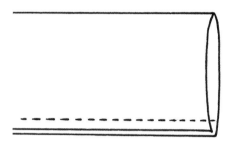

5 Hem the edges of the curtain: along one side edge of the curtain fabric, fold 1cm (⅜in) over to the wrong side then fold over another 2.5cm (1in). Stitch close to the edge of the fold. Repeat at the opposite edge of the curtain.

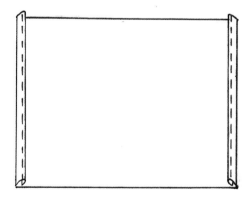

6 Hem the bottom of the curtain by repeating step 5 along the bottom edge of the curtain fabric.

Tip

If machine sewing the butterflies in place on the curtain, use an open front foot if you have one as it is easier to see when stitching.

7 Take one tab and fold it in half, with the seam on the inside. On the right side of the curtain, align the side of the tab with the edge of the curtain and the ends of the tab with the top unfinished edge of the curtain. Pin in place, then stitch across the tab, 5mm (¼in) from the edge.

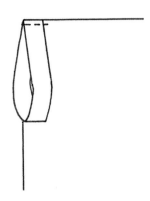

8 Attach another tab to the other side of your curtain as you did in step 7. Attach the remaining tabs at evenly spaced intervals along the top edge, aiming for a gap of approximately 13cm (5in) between each tab.

9 Take your additional curtain fabric strip and prepare as follows. At both short ends, fold 1.25cm (½in) and then 2.5cm (1in) over to the wrong side of the strip. Fold up 1.25cm (½in) to the wrong side on one long edge of the strip.

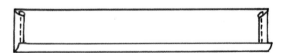

10 Align the top of the strip with the top of the curtain, right sides together, sandwiching the tabs between. Stitch through all the layers 1.25cm (½in) from the top edge. (This is done to encase/hide the raw edges of the tabs and the top of curtain.)

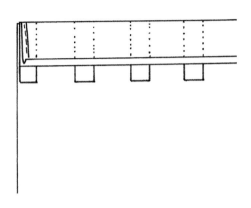

11 Fold the strip over the top of the curtain to the wrong side, then press. Stitch along close to the long folded edge of the attached strip.

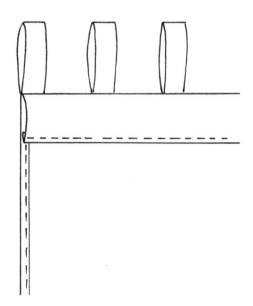

12 Tah dah! Your curtain is finished and ready to be hung.

Butterfly Bedroom

You can use the butterfly templates for all sorts of decorative applications in a little girl's bedroom to give her a butterfly-themed room, from curtains to lampshades. To make the wall decorations shown, use fabric glue to stick fabric off-cuts to pieces of card, then cut out some butterfly shapes in different sizes, and attach them to the wall with adhesive putty. A butterfly motif is also the perfect way to decorate a Holly scatter cushion – simply fuse your selected butterfly motif fabric to fusible webbing, then cut out your chosen butterfly shape from it. Fuse the butterfly to the front area of the cushion fabric and appliqué with blanket stitch before making the cushion.

Zoe Lampshade

What better way to light up a room in style than with a patterned, handmade lampshade? Choose your fabric to co-ordinate with your tiny one's bedroom, and have fun picking out her favourite colours. You could match the Lilly duvet and pillow set, or delightfully mismatch.

This shade could be on a bedside lamp or work as a drum shade in the centre of the room. Bespoke lampshades look so amazing and professional, you might even find yourself making a grown-up version for your own room…

You will need

For a 20cm (8in) diameter, 27cm (10½in) tall lampshade

Lampshade ring, 20cm (8in) diameter without light-bulb fitting

Lampshade ring, 20cm (8in) diameter with light-bulb fitting

Self-adhesive lampshade panel, at least 65 x 29cm (25½ x 11½in)

9mm (⅜in) double-sided tape

Fabric a little larger than the self-adhesive lampshade panel, at least 77.5 x 32cm (26½ x12½in)

FABRIC COLOUR NOTES

First a note about self-adhesive lampshade panel. It is a stiff/rigid PVC and one side has a self-adhesive with a backing paper that you peel off when you want to stick fabric to it. The panel can be covered with any fabric of your choosing. For my choice, I returned to the fabrics that I used in the Lilly duvet and pillow set, so as to give an overall theme to the bedroom. For the larger ceiling lamp I chose the fabric with the larger sized print that would let more light through. For the bedside table lamp I chose the more densely patterned print that will give a softer, more subdued 'bed-time-reading-atmosphere' light.

Cutting

- Self-adhesive lampshade panel: cut 65 x 29cm (25½ x 11½in).
- Fabric: cut 77.5 x 32cm (26½ x 12½in).

Tip

To make your choice of lampshade size: cut the self-adhesive lampshade panel so it is the circumference of your lampshade ring plus 1cm (⅜in) long by the desired height of your lampshade plus 2.5cm (1in), and cut your fabric so it is the circumference of the ring plus 4cm (1½in) by the desired height plus 5cm (2in).

Making

1 Take the lampshade panel and, on the side without the self-adhesive backing, score a line all along, 1cm (⅜in) from the top long edge. Use a craft knife and take care not to cut all the way through. Repeat 1cm (⅜in) from the bottom edge of the panel.

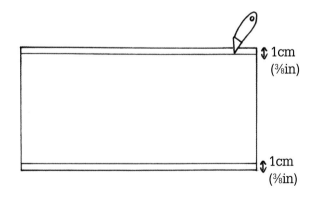

1cm (⅜in)

1cm (⅜in)

2 Iron your fabric and place it right side down on a flat surface. Peel the backing paper off the lampshade panel and position it in the centre of your fabric. Smooth with your hands, working outwards from the centre, sticking the panel to the wrong side of the fabric. Trim the excess fabric off all around, in line with the lampshade panel.

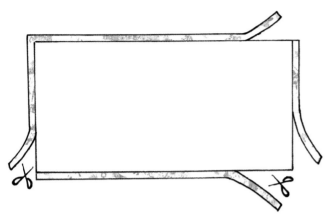

3 Crack the lampshade panel backing along the scored edge by bending it back and forth, and peel off the self-adhesive strip to reveal the fabric beneath. Repeat at opposite edge.

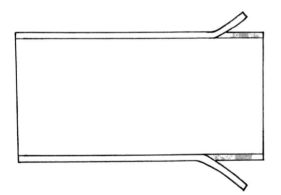

4 Stick a line of double-sided tape to the wrong side along one short edge of the fabric-backed lampshade panel.

tape

Tip

If you have a directional print fabric that you would like a certain way up when the lampshade is finished, ensure that the lampshade ring with the light-bulb fitting is inside the lampshade and positioned at the correct side.

5 Stick some double-sided tape to the outside edge of both the lampshade rings, keeping the ring in the centre of the tape. Peel the backing paper off the tape and curl the edges of the tape around the ring.

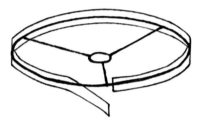

7 Peel the backing paper off the tape you applied in step 4 and overlap it onto the other end of the lampshade panel. With the join on a flat surface, press down hard on the join to stick it together.

8 Snip the fabric edge in line with the struts of the lampshade light-bulb fitting ring so that the fabric can fold past them. Fold the excess fabric edge around the ring towards the inside of the lampshade, keeping it stretched tight to avoid puckering. Push the fabric edges up behind the ring and smooth with the corner of a ruler. Repeat at the opposite end of the lampshade to complete your new bedroom accessory.

6 Starting at one end, place the sticky rings on the outer edges of the lampshade panel and, keeping the rings in line with the edges, roll them towards the other end, rolling the lampshade panel around the rings as you go.

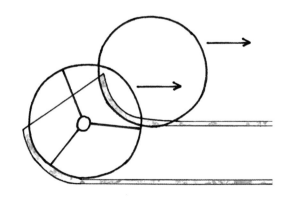

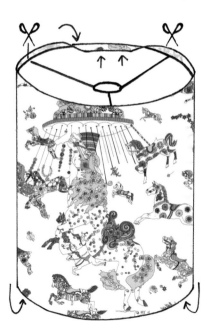

Butterfly Lampshade

A rainbow of butterflies float across this variation on the Zoe lampshade. Apply fusible webbing to fabric scraps and cut out your butterflies using the butterfly templates (see Templates). Fuse the butterflies to white fabric (appliqué optional) before sticking the fabric to the self-adhesive lampshade panel.

Isabel Baskets

I just love these stackable, collectible baskets. They are so practical, so very pretty, and sure to appeal to any little girl.

   Perfect for the top of her chest of drawers (too cute to be stashed away inside), they can be home for hair bands, necklaces, toy rabbits; whatever she treasures. She can use them to carry around projects or toys, which can then be tidied away easily at the end of the day. You can also make these baskets without handles – they're just as pretty and equally useful. She'll be thrilled!

You will need

For a big basket, 13cm (5in) tall by 18cm (7in) wide

Basket fabric, 33 x 43cm (13 x 17in)

Lining fabric, 33 x 42cm (13 x 16½in)

Handles fabric, 5 x 124.5cm (2 x 49in)

Medium-weight fusible interfacing, 5 x 124.5cm (2 x 49in)

Craft weight fusible interfacing, 33 x 43cm (13 x 17in)

Fusible wadding (batting), 33 x 43cm (13 x 17in)

For a small basket, 11cm (4½in) tall by 14cm (5½in) wide

Basket fabric: 25 x 34cm (10 x 13½in)

Lining fabric: 25 x 33cm (10 x 13in)

Handles fabric: 5 x 100cm (2 x 39in)

Medium-weight fusible interfacing, 5 x 100cm (2 x 39in)

Craft weight fusible interfacing, 25 x 34cm (10 x 13½in)

Fusible wadding (batting), 25 x 34cm (10 x 13½in)

FABRIC COLOUR NOTES

Here I chose two fabrics in the same print but in contrasting colourways, with quite a strong difference in colour or shade so that the handles show up well against the basket fabric. This project also requires a non-directional, all-over print, as on one side of the basket the fabric will be the other way up.

Making

1. Fuse the medium-weight interfacing to the wrong side of the handles fabric. Fold in half lengthways with right sides together. Stitch along the long edge with a 5mm (¼in) seam to make a tube.

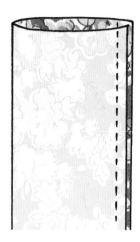

2. Turn the fabric tube right side out (see the Techniques section). (Note: the fabric tube is used to make both handles.)

3. Press the fabric tube flat with the seam running in the centre of one flat side. At one end of your flattened fabric tube, fold in 5mm (¼in) and press.

4 Form a continuous loop by pushing the other end of the flattened fabric tube about 5mm (¼in) into the folded end. Stitch the join through all the layers, about 3mm (⅛in) from the folded edge. This is now referred to as the 'handle loop'.

Tip

Ensure there are no twists in the handle loop before you join the ends.

5 To prepare the basket itself, first fuse the wadding (batting) to the wrong side of your basket fabric, then fuse the craft weight interfacing to the wadding (batting), following the manufacturer's instructions. If you are not using fusible products, tack (baste) all the layers together, sandwiching the wadding (batting) between the interfacing and the fabric. We'll refer to this sandwich of fabric, wadding (batting) and interfacing as the 'basket fabric' from this point onwards. Find the centre of the top (short edge) of your basket fabric, and mark with a pin or tailor's chalk. Find the centre of the side (long edge) and mark that too.

Tip

To find the centre of any piece of fabric you can measure or simply fold it in half.

6 Lay your basket fabric right side up on a flat surface. Check that your handle loop is flat, making sure the joining seam is in the middle. The following are the measurements for the big basket, if you are making the small one see the note at the end of this step. Lay the handle loop on top (seam side down) with the right-hand edge of the handle 3cm (1¼in) (a) from the top centre of the basket fabric. Align the joining seam of the handle with the (lengthways) centre of the basket 22cm (8½in) (b) from the top of the basket. Make sure the handle overhangs by equal lengths at the top and bottom of the basket fabric, by about 10cm (4in) (c) at each end. On the top layer of the handle loop, mark with a pin the point where the loop crosses the edge of the basket fabric. Pin the bottom handle loop to the basket fabric.

Note: the measurements for the smaller basket are (a) 2.5cm (1in), (b) 17cm (6¾in), and (c) 7.5cm (3in).

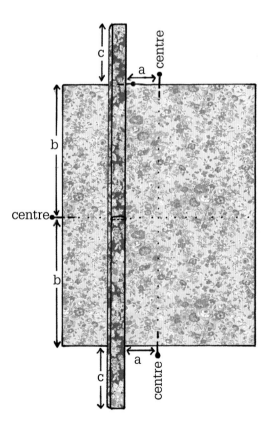

7 Using co-ordinating thread, stitch 2mm (¹⁄₁₆in) from the edges of either side of the handle loop, stopping 2.5cm (1in) from the top and bottom edges of the basket fabric.

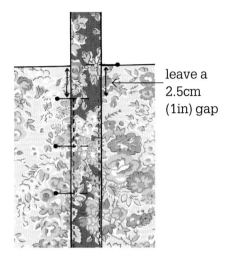

leave a 2.5cm (1in) gap

8 Lay the other side of the handle loop 3cm (1¼in) from the centre, aligning your pin (d) from step 6 with the top of the basket fabric. Stitch as you did in step 7.

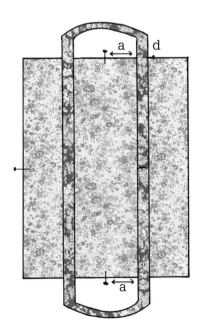

9 Fold the basket fabric in half, right sides together, and stitch together at the sides with a 1cm (³⁄₈in) seam. Draw a line along the bottom fold to mark the bottom centre. Press the side seams open.

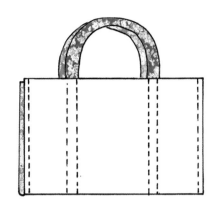

10 Working at one edge, squash the side seam down to meet the bottom of the basket. Align your bottom centre (drawn) line and side seam together at (f). Squash the side seam down to meet the bottom of the basket. Draw a line (e) across the corner and sew. For the bigger basket, this line must be 14cm (5½in) (g) from edge to edge and at right angles to side seam (f). Side seam (f) is equidistant from the edges at (e), with 5.5cm (2¼in) (h) each side. Sew across the corner along line (e), and trim the corner off 1cm (³⁄₈in) from line (e). If you are making the smaller basket the measurements are: (g) 5cm (2in) and (h) 10cm (4in).

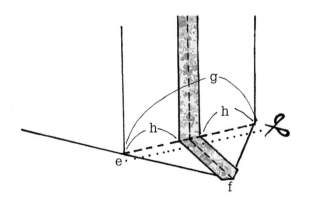

11 Repeat step 10 at the other edge of the basket.

12 Turn right side out, pushing the corners out with the end of a pencil.

13 Sew the basket lining following steps 9 to 11. (Do not turn inside out.)

14 Insert the basket into the lining, with right sides together. It will be a tight fit – the lining may need some persuasion to stretch a bit! Ensure the handles are folded down and pushed away from the top edge.

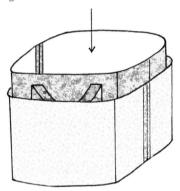

15 Align the top edges of the lining and the basket, then align the side seams too. Pin all around the top, or tack (baste) if you prefer. Stitch with a 1cm (⅜in) seam around the top, leaving a 14cm (5½in) gap.

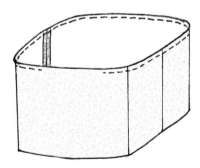

16 Turn right side out, pulling the basket through the gap. Again, you may find that a bit of persuasion is necessary!

17 To close the gap, fold over 1cm (⅜in) of the basket and 1cm (⅜in) of the lining and slip stitch or ladder stitch together (see Hand sewing stitches in the Techniques section). Press the basket, pressing the lining down, away from the top edge. Pin in place and, using co-ordinating thread, topstitch all around the top of the basket 1cm (⅜in) from the top edge.

18 Stitch the handles to the basket in an 'X' pattern Enjoy your basket!

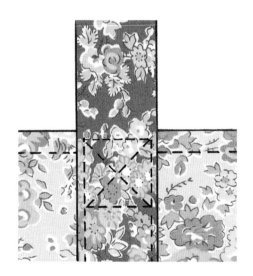

Tip

*For a simple basket – perhaps to be used
as a toy tidy – there's no need to add
handles. Make life even easier and just
follow steps 5 and 9 to 17.*

Twirly Girly Garments

It feels great making clothes for kids and seeing them run around in your creations – especially when it's this simple, and the results are so pretty.

My daughter is over the moon whenever I make her something, whether it's a simple t-shirt dress or fancy party skirt. I have been known to whip up one of the following projects in a party panic, as they are really just a rectangle of fabric, sewn in straight lines. These party pieces are as beginner friendly as they come!

Any of these three projects will be eagerly received – they combine colour, texture and prints to make something very special.

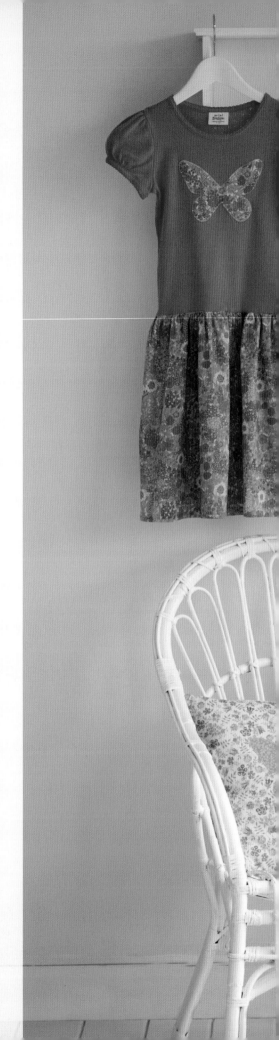

Fleur Embellished Party Skirt

This is my modern take on the kind of heavily embellished, traditional skirt worn with pride on special occasions by girls and women from different cultures across the world.

If, like me, you have a closely guarded stash of ribbons, this is a great way to dip into your collection. Take time to enjoy putting different combinations together, to create your very own heirloom masterpiece. It's surprising how easy it is to create such a show-stopper skirt.

You will need

For a finished skirt 38cm (15in) long

Cotton lawn or lightweight fabric, 46 x 137cm (18 x 54in)

Ruffle fabrics: two strips of 2.5 x 137cm (1 x 54in) co-ordinating fabric (see Tip)

8–10 different ribbons in a variety of widths and textures: satin, sheer, organza, glitter, ric rac, lace etc, which when laid out next to each other give a total width of 15cm (6in).

Buttonhole elastic or regular elastic, 65cm (26in) of 2cm (¾in) wide

Button, size suitable for your elastic (only needed if using buttonhole elastic)

To customize the skirt size

Fabric: measure from the child's waist to the desired hem length of the skirt (above or below knee, you choose!) then add 7.5cm (3in) to this measurement. This is the length of 137cm (54in) wide fabric you will need.

Elastic: measure the child's waist and add 7.5cm (3in).

Tip

To make the thin ruffle strips, take 137cm (54in) wide fabric and make a snip in the fabric and rip or tear it to give a straight edge (don't cut with scissors); snip and rip again at 2.5cm (1in) so you have lightly frayed edges.

FABRIC COLOUR NOTES

Pick out one colour from your fabric and choose ribbons in varying shades of this colour. Or you could mix it up and choose different colours picked out from your fabric. For my ribbon choice I used 5.5cm (2¼in) wide crinkled taffeta, ric rac, 1.25cm (½in) wide satin, 1cm (⅜in) glitter ribbon, 2.5cm (1in) wide organza, 2.5cm (1in) wide cotton lace, and two different shades of 1.25cm (½in) wide satin ribbons, all in varying shades of purple.

Tip

Use the measurements given in the You will need list to make a skirt that will fit an average height 6–7 year old just below the knee, or mid calf for the average 5–6 year old and ankle length for the average 3–4 year old.

Making

1 Take the ruffle fabric strips and, with right sides together, stitch the two short ends to make one long strip.

2 Sew two rows of long tacking (basting) stitches 1cm (⅜in) apart. Leave long threads at both ends. Take hold of a set of long thread ends (one each from the same end, same side of both rows of stitches) and pull to create a gather. Ease the fabric along the stitches to even out the gather.

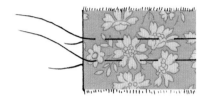

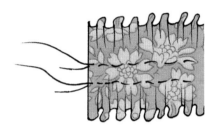

3 Adjust the gather until the length of the ruffle is reduced to 137cm (54in).

4 Lay the skirt fabric out on a table and experiment with the arrangement of the ribbons. To follow my design, place the widest ribbon at the bottom with the ruffle in the centre, then the ric rac. When you are happy with your design, take a picture or make notes of the order of the ribbons.

5 Stitch the ribbons on (instructions now follow for my ribbon arrangement). Starting with your bottom (widest) ribbon lay it on your skirt fabric 4cm (1½in) from the bottom edge, pin in place. Stitch it to the skirt using co-ordinating thread, close to the edge of the ribbon. Lay the ruffle centred on top. Stitch in place along the centre of the ruffle, between the tacking (basting) stitches. Remove the tacking (basting) stitches. Next lay the ric rac on top of the centre of the ruffle and stitch in place.

6 Then lay the next ribbon above the wide ribbon, overlapping the wide ribbon edge. Stitch close to the edge through this ribbon and wide ribbon. Repeat with subsequent ribbons, always overlapping the top ribbon over the previous one, sewing through both.

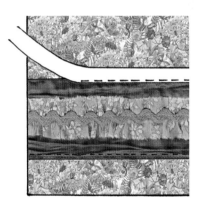

7 With right sides together, form the skirt loop and stitch the edges together with a 1cm (⅜in) seam. Finish the seam (see Techniques section) and press to one side. This is the back seam of the skirt.

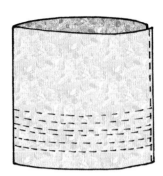

8 Hem the bottom edge of the skirt by folding up 1.25cm (½in), and pressing. Fold another 2cm (1in) over, and press again. Stitch all around the hem, 2mm (⅛in) from the top fold.

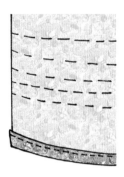

9 Fold over 1.25cm (½in) at the top of the skirt and press.

10 If not using buttonhole elastic, go straight to step 11. Make a 2cm (¾in) buttonhole (see Techniques section) 5mm (¼in) from the top folded edge of the skirt, stitching through the folded edge.

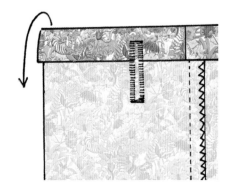

11 Fold over another 3cm (1¼in) at the top of the skirt. Stitch in place close to the fold, all around the skirt. Note: if you are not using buttonhole elastic, leave a 4cm (1½in) gap.

12 Machine zigzag stitch over the ends of the elastic to prevent fraying; alternatively, you can blanket stitch by hand (see Hand sewing stitches in the Techniques section). Attach a safety pin to one end and insert the elastic into the waistband through the buttonhole (or through the gap if not using buttonhole elastic). Push the elastic around through the waistband with your thumbs and forefingers. Note: secure the other end of the elastic with another safety pin once it is nearly at the buttonhole/gap so that it does not disappear into waistband. Make sure the elastic lies flat within the waistband.

13 If you are not using buttonhole elastic, omit this step and go to step 15. Pull the safety pin out of the buttonhole, pulling the elastic about 7.5cm (3in) out of the buttonhole. Adjust the other end of the elastic so that it sits just inside the buttonhole, and pin it in place (take care not to let go and lose it!). Secure the elastic in place, stitching through all the layers close to the buttonhole using machine zigzag stitch or blanket stitch by hand.

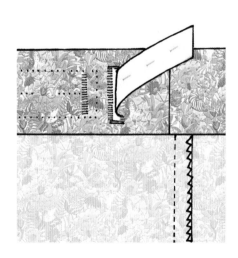

14 Stitch the button in place, close to the buttonhole. Adjust the elastic to the desired length and push a buttonhole over the button. The fitting of your skirt made using buttonhole elastic is now complete.

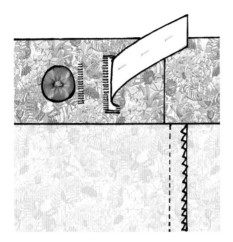

15 To complete the fitting of the skirt if you are using plain elastic, pull both ends of elastic about 7.5cm (3in) out of the gap and tie in a knot at the required waist measurement (about 59cm (23in) for 5–7 year olds). Slip stitch the gap closed (see Hand sewing stitches in the Techniques section). As your child grows these stitches can be undone and the elastic length adjusted to a different size or replaced.

Fleur with No Frills

If the party is this afternoon and the pressure is too much, or even if you just prefer a simpler look, you can make a plain version of this skirt without the embellishments – it's still very pretty if you pick the right fabric!

Libby Ra-ra Skirt

Who doesn't love a ra-ra skirt? I know I did, and still maintain a fondness for its flouncy delights. I was definitely a child of the 80s, and don't want my daughter to miss out on this particular cultural icon. This easy-to-make version is great for twirling at parties, or just in your living room.

You could mix it up with rainbow shades, graduate the tones or use your little one's favourite colours. Floral prints in popping colours are the perfect match for energetic tiny people.

You will need

For a finished skirt 35cm (14in) long

Top ruffle and waistband, 20 x 137cm (8 x 54in) cotton lawn or lightweight fabric

Middle ruffle, 24 x 137cm (9½ x 54in) cotton lawn or lightweight fabric

Bottom ruffle, 35 x 137cm (13¾ x 54in) cotton lawn or lightweight fabric

55cm (26in) of 2cm (¾in) wide elastic, either buttonhole elastic or regular

Button, size suitable for your elastic (only needed if using buttonhole elastic)

To customize the skirt size

Fabric: measure from child's waist to the desired hem length of the longest ruffle of the skirt (above or below knee, you choose!) then add 7.5cm (3in) to this measurement. This is the length of 137cm (54in) wide fabric you will need for the bottom ruffle

Elastic: measure the child's waist and add 7.5cm (3in)

Cutting

- Cut a 9cm (3½in) strip off the top ruffle/waistband fabric.

Tip

Using regular 122cm (44in) wide fabric works just as well, but results in a slightly less ruffled skirt.

Making

1 Start by making the top ruffle. Form a loop, with right sides together, and stitch the edges together with a 1cm (³⁄₈in) seam. Finish the seam and press to one side. Repeat with the 9cm (3½in) strip to make the waistband, and with the other two fabrics for the middle and bottom ruffles.

2 To hem the top ruffle, fold up 5mm (¼in) on one edge and then press. Fold another 1.25cm (½in) over and press again. Stitch all around the hem 2mm (¹⁄₁₆in) from the fold. Repeat with the other two ruffle pieces.

3 Make a gather on the middle ruffle all around the circumference at a distance of 12.5cm (5in) from the bottom hemmed edge. To do this, sew two rows of long tacking (basting) stitches 1cm (³⁄₈in) apart. You can do this on your sewing machine by setting the stitch length to about 4.5, or sew by hand. Leave long threads at both ends. Take hold of a set of long thread ends (one each from the same end, same side of both rows of stitches) and pull to create a gather. Ease the fabric along the stitches to even out the gathering, until the circumference is reduced to about 90cm (36in) long (or 45cm/18in when skirt is folded flat).

4 Sew regular length zigzag stitches around the circumference between the tacking (basting) rows. Remove the tacking (basting) stitches. Repeat with the bottom ruffle, 15cm (6in) from the bottom edge.

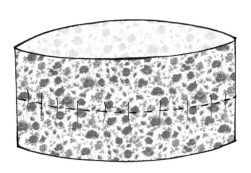

5 Insert the middle and then the bottom ruffle inside the top ruffle loop. Align the top edges, pin in place and stitch together 1cm (³⁄₈in) from the top edge.

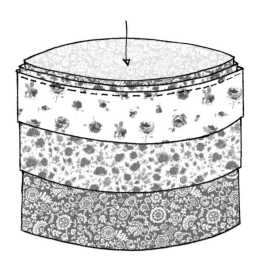

6 On one long edge of the waistband strip (see Cutting), fold up 1.25cm (½in) to the wrong side and press.

7 If not using buttonhole elastic, omit this step and go to step 8. Make a 2cm (¾in) buttonhole (see Techniques) 5mm (¼in) from the top folded edge of the waistband, stitching through the folded edge.

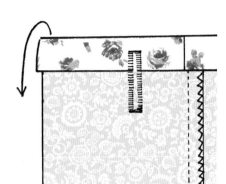

8 Turn the skirt from step 5 inside out and insert into the waistband loop, aligning the top edges (the non folded edge of the waistband). Pin and stitch together with a 1.25cm (½in) seam. Trim to 5mm (¼in) and finish the seam.

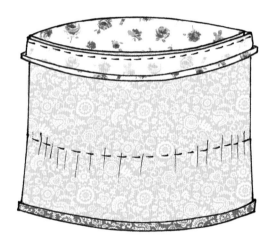

9 Turn the skirt right side out. Fold the waistband over the top edge of the skirt, ensuring that the folded waistband edge covers your stitching from step 7. Stitch 2mm (1/16in) from the folded edge all around the top of the skirt. Leave a 4cm (1½in) gap if you are not using buttonhole elastic.

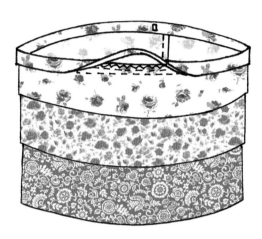

10 Machine zigzag stitch over the ends of the elastic to prevent fraying; alternatively, blanket stitch by hand (see Hand sewing stitches in the Techniques section). Attach a safety pin to one end and insert the elastic into the waistband through the buttonhole (or through the gap if not using buttonhole elastic). Push the elastic around through the waistband with your thumbs and forefingers. Note: secure the other end of the elastic with another safety pin once it is nearly at the buttonhole/gap so that it does not disappear into the waistband. Make sure the elastic lies flat within the waistband.

11 If you are not using buttonhole elastic, omit this step and go to step 13. Pull the safety pin out of the buttonhole, pulling the elastic about 7.5cm (3in) out of the buttonhole. Adjust the other end of the elastic so that it sits just inside the buttonhole, and pin it in place (take care not to let go and lose it!). Secure the elastic in place, stitching through all the layers close to the buttonhole using machine zigzag stitch or blanket stitch by hand (see Hand sewing stitches in the Techniques section).

12 Stitch the button in place, close to the buttonhole. Adjust the elastic to the desired length and push a buttonhole over the button. The fitting of your skirt made using buttonhole elastic is now complete.

13 To complete the fitting of the skirt if you are using plain elastic, pull both ends of elastic about 7.5cm (3in) out of the gap and tie in a knot at the required waist measurement (about 59cm (23in) for 5–7 year olds). Slip stitch the gap closed (see Hand sewing stitches in the Techniques section).

Tip

If you are using plain elastic, leave some spare in the waistband so that in the future you can open the stitched gap, undo the knot and adjust the elastic length, or even replace it, if a different size is required.

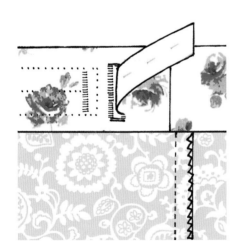

Hannah T-shirt Dress

This gorgeous little dress is cute enough for parties, but hard-wearing enough for everyday play. My daughter loves telling her friends that her mummy made it – while spinning around with delight.

Find a plain t-shirt in a fun colour, add a skirt made from one rectangular piece of fabric, and a matching butterfly appliqué if you feel so inclined... remember, using a light cotton lawn will give the skirt the all-important twirl factor.

And *voilà*, you have a gorgeous little dress, perfect for days in or days out.

You will need

For a t-shirt dress adapted to fit

Plain t-shirt

Cotton lawn or lightweight fabric 137cm (54in) wide, measure from child's waist to desired hem length of skirt (above or below knee, you choose!) then add 7.5cm (3in)

Scrap of matching fabric for appliqué, about 15 x 10cm (6 x 4in)

Medium or lightweight fusible interfacing, 15 x 10cm (6 x 4in)

Making

1 To prepare the appliqué fabric, follow the manufacturer's instructions and fuse the interfacing to the wrong side of the fabric scrap.

2 Cut out a butterfly from this fabric using the butterfly template (see Templates).

3 Position the butterfly centrally on the front of the t-shirt. Fix in place by tacking (basting), pinning or using washable glue. Hand stitch the butterfly to the t-shirt all around the edge using blanket stitch (see Hand sewing stitches in the Techniques section) or use machine zigzag stitch.

FABRIC COLOUR NOTES

I wanted a bright fun look for this skirt. I actually had more choice of fabric than with the t-shirt colour, so in this case the t-shirt came first. I picked a fabric with quite a few colours that didn't actually feature the exact shade of the t-shirt but went well with the overall theme of the fabric. If I'd started out with the fabric I could have picked out the pink, the turquoise or the green for the t-shirt.

4 Finish the long top edge of the skirt fabric with zigzag stitch.

5 To form the skirt loop, with right sides together, stitch the ends together with a 1cm (⅜in) seam. Finish the seam and press to one side. This is the back seam of the skirt.

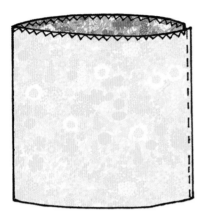

6 Hem the bottom edge of the skirt by folding up 1.25cm (½in), and press. Fold another 2.5cm (1in) over, and press again. Stitch all around the hem, 2mm (¹⁄₁₆in) from the top fold.

7 Next gather the top edge of the skirt. To do this, sew two rows of long tacking (basting) stitches 1cm (⅜in) apart. The top row needs to be 1cm (⅜in) from the top finished edge of the skirt. You can do this on your sewing machine by setting the stitch length to about 4.5, or sew by hand. Leave long thread ends at both ends. Take hold of a set of long threads (one each from the same end, same side of both rows of stitches) and pull to create a gather.

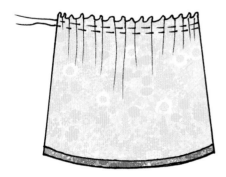

8 Ease the fabric along the stitches to even out the gather, until the length is reduced to match the circumference of the t-shirt.

Tip
For an average height 6–7 year old, the measurement from the shoulder to the waist seam will be about 36cm (14in).

9 Measure from the child's shoulder to just below the waist. Mark this distance, measured from the shoulder seam on the t-shirt, with a pin.

10 With right sides together, insert the t-shirt into the upside-down skirt. Line the finished edge of the skirt up with the pin from step 9. Adjust the gather to fit the t-shirt if necessary. Ensure the skirt top edge is parallel with the bottom of the t-shirt. Pin or tack in place. Stitch the skirt to the t-shirt all around the circumference in the middle of the gather tacking (basting) stitches. Remove the tacking (basting) stitches.

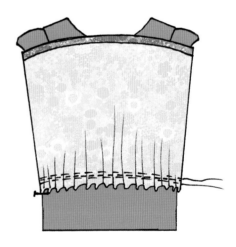

11 Turn the skirt right side out and you're done.

Pretty Little Things

In this section you'll find the projects that are quickest to create, making them a swift hit of creative loveliness. A few, like the Mia doll, require a little more effort but are well worth it. Bags, belts, pencil cases, scrunchies, dolls, bracelets, rosettes… all in brilliant prints and happy colours. Little-girl paradise, in other words.

As a child I would have gone pretty crazy for any of these projects, and I don't think too much has changed. If you are in need of ideas for a simple but special gift, then you've come to the right place.

Molly Purse

This mini version of a grown-up classic quilted bag is just too cool for school. Definitely the thing for an outing, a party or a trip to town. It looks special but is deceptively practical. It is roomy enough to hold lots of bits and bobs, and the lucky owner won't lose it thanks to the pretty plaited cross-body strap. The button detail keeps everything secure.

Ponies, flowers or whatever she loves – use your fabric choice to reflect her personality, and you'll have a hit on your hands.

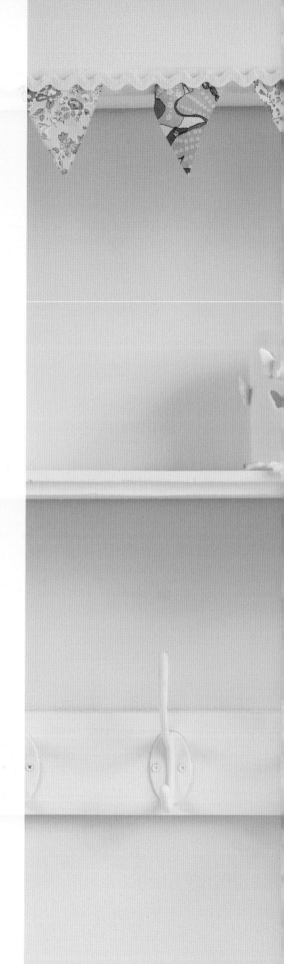

You will need

For a 18 x 14cm (7 x 5½in) bag

Outer fabric, one fat quarter or 46 x 55cm (18 x 22in)

Lining fabric, one fat quarter or 46 x 55cm (18 x 22in)

Wadding (batting), 28 x 43cm (11 x 17in) (optionally fusible and with printed grid)

Self-cover button, 2.5cm (1in) diameter

Cutting

- Outer fabric, lining and wadding (batting): cut a piece 28 x 43cm (11 x 17in) of each.

- For the button loop: cut a piece 4 x 7.5cm (1½ x 3in) from remaining outer fabric.

- For the plaited handle: cut three pieces 4 x 46cm (1½ x 18in) from the remaining outer fabric, and cut six pieces 4 x 46cm (1½ x 18in) from the remaining lining fabric.

Making

1 First, prepare the quilted fabric for the purse outer. If you are using fusible wadding (batting) with a printed grid, fuse to the wrong side of the outer fabric. If you have non-fusible wadding (batting), tack (baste) it or use fabric adhesive to secure the wadding (batting) to the wrong side of the outer fabric. Draw lines (using pencil or washable fabric pen) 3cm (1¼in) apart at 45 degrees across the fabric. At right angles to these lines, draw lines 3cm (1¼in) apart to make a diamond-like grid. Now quilt the wadding (batting) to the fabric: stitch using straight stitch, following the marked grid lines, all over the fabric.

2 Using the purse template (see Templates), cut one Molly purse pattern piece out of the quilted fabric you prepared in step 1, and another one from the lining fabric.

3 Take the button loop fabric, fold it in half along the length, right sides together, and sew with a 5mm (¼in) seam along the long edge to make a tube.

4 Turn the button loop fabric right side out, (see instructions in the Techniques section). Press, then fold the button loop fabric in half and align the ends at the top centre of the purse outer on right side of the fabric, with the loop pointing in towards purse. Secure in place, stitching 5mm (¼in) from the top edge.

5 Place the quilted purse piece from step 2, right side up, on a flat surface. Place the lining on top, right sides together. Pin around the edges and stitch together with a 1cm (³⁄₈in) seam, leaving a 7.5cm (3in) gap open at the bottom.

6 Clip the curves and trim the corners of any excess fabric as shown.

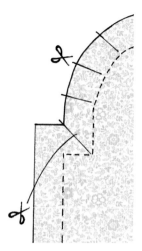

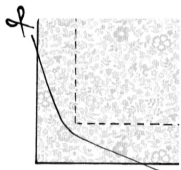

7 Turn right side out and press. Turn the seam allowance in and close the gap with slip stitch (see Hand sewing stitches in the Techniques section).

8 With the outer sides together, fold up the bottom of the purse along the fold line (shown on the template). Stitch together along the side seams, with a 1cm (⅜in) seam. Turn right sides out and press.

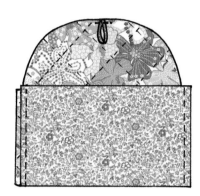

9 Sew the button in place on the front side, where the loop meets the front of the purse.

Tip

self-cover buttons are available in plastic and metal in a range of different sizes, and they enable you to make a button to perfectly match your project.

10 For the plaited handle, stitch three of the lining fabric strips together at the short ends, right sides together, with a 1cm (³⁄₈in) seam, to make one long piece measuring of 134cm (53in). Trim the seams to reduce bulk and press them open.

11 Follow steps 3 and 4 to make a thin tube or fabric ribbon. Slip stitch (or machine stitch) closed at both ends.

12 Repeat steps 10 and 11 with the remaining three pieces of lining fabric and the three pieces of outer fabric to give you three long fabric ribbons.

13 Tie the ribbons together with an overhand knot about 2.5cm (1in) from the ends. Plait the three ribbons together, then tie a knot at the other end of the plait, leaving 2.5cm (1in) tails.

Tip

Pin a safety pin through the first knot of your ribbons and, so you have something to pull against while you're plaiting, then attach it another surface, for example, the cover on your ironing board or the arm of your sofa.

14 Finally, attach the strap: on the back of the purse pin the strap in place, placing the knot in the top left corner, 1.25cm (½in) from the side and 1.25cm (½in) from folded top edge. Place the other end of the strap at the opposite top corner of the purse, ensuring there are no twists. Secure in place with three rows of stitching on top of each other, just above the knot. Repeat with three rows of stitching below the knot. Your bag is finished.

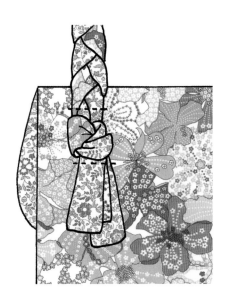

Orla Pencil Cases

I was obsessed with stationery when I was little, and hoarded pens, rulers and rubbers in my favourite pencil case. Here I show you how to make a gorgeous zipped case that is good enough to hold even the most special collection.

This project is a great way to use your treasured stash of fabric scraps, as the pieces are so small – when finished, they are just one inch square. If you don't have a stash, this is a great, colourful project to build up a little collection for.

You will need

For a 23 x 13cm (9 x 5in) pencil case

For the quilted case

Outer fabric: two pieces of cotton fabric, each 24 x 14cm (9½ x 5½in)

For the patchwork case

45 different rainbow coloured cotton fabric scraps, minimum size 5 x 5cm (2 x 2in). See Fabric Colour Notes below.

For both cases

Lining fabric: two pieces, each 24 x 14cm (9½ x 5½in)

Wadding (batting): two pieces, each 24 x 14cm (9½ x 5½in) (optionally fusible and with printed grid for the quilted version)

Zip, 23cm (9in)

FABRIC COLOUR NOTES

For the patchwork version of the pencil case I delved through my stash of scraps and pulled out fabrics to create a rainbow effect. I used: 10 red/dark pink mix, five pale pink, five yellow, five green, five turquoise, five blue, five pale purple and five purple.

Cutting

- Patchwork version: cut two 4cm (1½in) squares of each of the 45 different fabric scraps.

All seam allowances are 5mm (¼in) unless otherwise stated.

Preparing the Pencil Case Outsides

For the quilted version

1 Prepare the quilted fabric for the pencil case outer. If you are using fusible wadding (batting) with a printed grid, fuse to the wrong side of the outer fabric. If using non-fusible wadding (batting), tack (baste) or use fabric adhesive to secure it to the wrong side of the outer fabric. Draw lines (using pencil or washable fabric pen) 3cm (1¼in) apart at 45 degrees across the fabric. At right angles to these lines, draw lines 3cm (1¼in) apart to make a diamond-like grid. Quilt the wadding (batting) to the fabric: stitch using straight stitch, following the marked grid lines, all over the fabric.

2 From the quilted fabric cut two pieces 23 x 13cm (9 x 5in). These are your outer pencil case pieces. Now skip to Completing the Pencil Cases.

For the patchwork version

1 Take one set of your 45 squares and arrange the colours in nine vertical columns of five, having the lightest shades at the top, through to the darkest at the bottom.

2 Stitch the columns of five together in order: start by placing a top square on a second square, right sides together, and stitch them together along one edge. Open out, then add the next colour in the same way, continuing with the remaining squares to give a row of five squares.

3 Arrange the columns from left to right in rainbow order: red, dark pink, pale pink, yellow, green, turquoise, blue, pale purple and purple. So that the seams will fit together smoothly when you stitch the columns together, press the red row seams up, the dark pink row down, the pale pink row up and continue alternating the seam direction through the rest of the rows.

4 Stitch the rows together in rainbow order. This is one of your patchwork outer pieces.

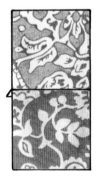

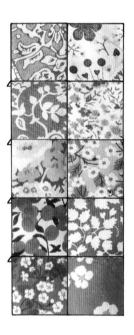
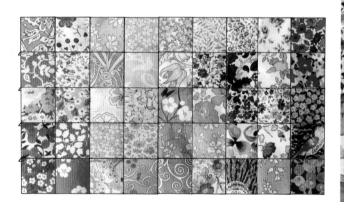

Tip
If you prefer, you can stitch the squares
together in any random order from step 2.

5 Repeat steps 1 to 4 with the other set of 45 squares, but in step 3 order them from right to left to complete the second of your patchwork outer pieces.

6 Trim your patchwork outer pieces to 24 x 14cm (9½ x 5½in).

7 Fix one wadding (batting) piece to the wrong side of each of the patchwork outer pieces using washable glue or by tacking (basting). Repeat with the other patchwork outer. These are your exterior pencil case pieces.

Completing the Pencil Cases

1 Place the zip, right side down, on the right side of one of your pencil case outer pieces, aligning the zip edge with the top edge. Pin it in place then stitch the zip to the pencil case outer piece along top edge, close to the zip.

Tip
Use the zipper foot on your sewing machine to make life much easier!

2 Place one piece of lining fabric right side down on top of the outer piece, right sides together, sandwiching the zip between the layers. Pin and then sew along the top edge, close to the zip.

3 Trim the ends of the zip level with the edges of the fabric and open out.

4 Repeat steps 1 and 2 with the other outer piece and lining on the opposite side of the zip. (The diagram shows the second pencil case outer piece having been stitched in place, as in step 1.)

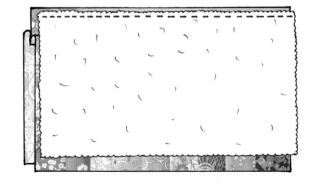

5 Open out so that you have both lining pieces on one side and the outer pieces on the other side of the zip, all right sides together. Open the zip halfway.

6 Starting at the bottom of the lining, with right sides together, sew the front and backs of the pencil case together, sewing continuously around the edges but leaving a gap of about 8cm (3in) at the bottom of the lining.

7 Turn right side out by reaching in and pulling the pencil case through the gap in the bottom of lining, pulling the lining right side out as well. Slip stitch or ladder stitch the lining bottom pieces together (see Hand sewing stitches in the Techniques section) to close the gap. Push the lining into the bag. Press.

8 Fill with a rainbow of coloured pencils, and you have a gorgeous gift!

Sara Drawstring Bag

This might just be the most versatile project in this book – and of course it's easy too. A multi-use stash bag or travel bag, toy bag or shoe bag, personalized with her own monogram. Packing her favourite toys to go stay with Granny never felt such fun!

Use complementary shades as I have done here, or mix it up with contrasting brights. Mums may find themselves borrowing this bag a little too often, so you might like to make a few extra for yourself in different prints. It's also a great, practical gift project.

You will need

For a 25 x 29cm (10 x 11½in) bag

Outer fabric, one fat quarter or 46 x 55cm (18 x 22in)

Fabric scrap for monogram, about 13 x 15cm (5 x 6in)

Lightweight fusible interfacing, two pieces each 13 x 15cm (5 x 6in)

FABRIC COLOUR NOTES

If this bag is a present, pick the recipient's favourite colour. The letter fabric needs to be several shades darker than that used for the bag, so try out a strip of your intended letter fabric against the bag fabric to check that it will show up. I chose the fabric to be the same colour as the letter, for a matching look.

Cutting

- Bag: cut a piece 33 x 55cm (13 x 22in).
- Drawstring: cut one piece 4 x 55cm (1½ x 22in) and one piece 4 x 11.5cm (1½ x 4½in), or just one piece 4 x 66cm (1½ x 26½in) if using 137cm (54in) wide Liberty fabric.

Making

1 To make the drawstring, stitch both of your 4cm (1½in) wide pieces together, right sides together, at the short ends, with a 1.25cm (½in) seam, to make one long piece (there's no need to do this if you're using Liberty fabric). Trim the seams and press open. Cut to 66cm (26½in) long.

2 Fold the strip in half along the length, right sides together, and sew with a 5mm (¼in) seam along the long edge to make a tube. Turn the drawstring fabric tube right side out, (see the instructions in the Techniques section). Press the drawstring flat with the seam running in the centre of one flat side. At the ends of your drawstring, fold in 5mm (¼in) to the inside of the fabric tube and press. Slip stitch (or machine stitch) closed at both ends.

3 To prepare the monogram, iron one piece of fusible interfacing to the wrong side of your scrap of fabric. Print and cut out your chosen letter or monogram. Pin your paper letter to your fabric scrap, draw round in pencil and cut it out. Cut your other piece of interfacing so it is about 1.25cm (½in) bigger all round than your letter.

Tip

Pick a font on your computer and print out your letter to use as a template. I used the font Arial Rounded MT Bold, size 500.

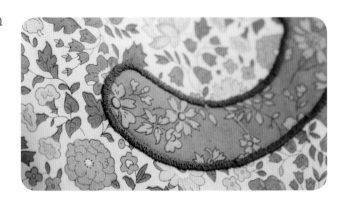

Sara Drawstring Bag

4 Fold your bag fabric in half, wrong sides together, and position your letter in the centre of one side of your bag, on the right side. Use washable glue or tack (baste) in place. Open the bag fabric out and fuse the other piece of interfacing behind the letter on the wrong side of your bag fabric. On the right side sew all around the monogram with satin stitch or blanket stitch (see Hand sewing stitches in the Techniques section) or use your sewing machine.

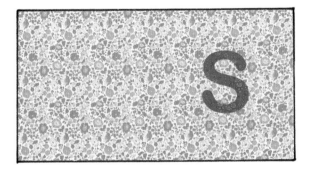

5 Finish the raw edges using zigzag stitch (see Finishing a seam in the Techniques section) all around the fabric. Fold over 5mm (¼in) at the top edge, and press. Fold over another 2.5cm (1in) and press again. Open out the folds. (It is easier to iron at this stage before making the bag.)

6 Fold your bag fabric in half lengthways, right sides together. Using a 1.25cm (½in) seam, stitch the bottom and side edges together, stopping 7.5cm (3in) from the top edge. Back stitch to secure the end of the seam.

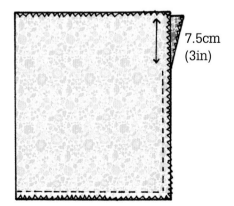

7.5cm (3in)

7 Fold the seam allowance back on each side, above where you stopped stitching in step 6, and press. Stitch 2mm (¹⁄₁₆in) from the fold.

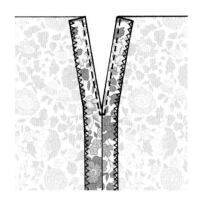

8 Fold 5mm (¼in) over at the top edge and fold over another 2.5cm (1in). Stitch 2mm (¹⁄₁₆in) from the fold, through all the layers, all around the bag to make the casing for the drawstring.

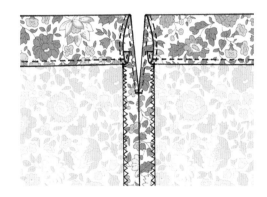

9 Turn the bag right side out. Attach a safety pin to one end of your drawstring and feed it through the casing at the top of your bag. Bring the ends of the drawstring together and tie in an overhand knot. You've finished!

Gwen Belt

It's really hard to find pretty belts in fun colours, so why not make your own? I really enjoy making these belts as presents for my daughter's friends. They are an unusual, thoughtful, yet practical gift for all sorts of ages. Since the size is adjustable, growth spurts present no problems!

Try creating a reversible version, for maximum versatility. You could co-ordinate the belt with a specific dress or trousers, but you don't have to – any outfit will be gorgeously accessorized.

You will need

For a belt adapted to fit

Cotton fabric, 7.5cm (3in) wide x length of webbing plus 2.5cm (1in)

Webbing: 2.5cm (1in) wide canvas/ polypropylene webbing, for length measure child's waist and add 10cm (4in)

Two 27mm (1in) D-rings

FABRIC COLOUR NOTES

Choose any colour for this belt. If you would like to make a reversible belt, you can use two great colours to complement a wide range of outfits, or provide a funky contrast. Just sew two pieces of fabric 5cm (2in) wide and the length of your webbing plus 2.5cm (1in), right sides together, along the long edge with a 1.25cm (½in) seam. Then follow the Making instructions.

Tip
For an average size six year old, the cut fabric size is 7.5 x 73cm (3 x 29in).

Making

1 Fold 1cm (³⁄₈in) in along one long edge of one piece of fabric and press.

2 With the right side up, overlap the right-hand edge of the fabric 1cm (³⁄₈in) over the long left-hand edge of the webbing, letting the fabric overhang at the top edge by 1.25cm (½in). Stitch the fabric to the webbing along the whole length.

3 Wrap the fabric tightly around the webbing.

Gwen Belt

4 Fold the top edge down by 1.25cm (½in). Repeat at the other end of the fabric.

6 At one end of the belt fold 2.5cm (1in) over, through the two D-rings. Stitch along the end of the belt three times, and it's ready to wear.

5 Wrap the fabric tightly around the webbing and stitch through all the layers, along the length of the fabric, close to the fold you made in step 1. Stitch along the top and bottom edges and the other long side of the belt.

Tip
Before stitching, take time to check that the top and bottom edges are straight and ensure the folds in the corners are neat, and that any folds or edges are tucked away.

Mia Doll

Little ones will love discovering that Mia has both a serious and a fun side. Sometimes she is a Little Lady, like a rose garden, proper and just-so... but flip her over and she becomes a Wild Flower, like a wild garden, letting her hair down and running free! She's just waiting to go on adventures and become part of all kinds of stories.

Mia harks back to vintage dolls, but has a fresh modern look. Be creative by using contrasting fabrics and trims – you'll love the beautiful result.

You will need

For a 40cm (16in) tall doll

Plain fabric for body: 46 x 40.5cm (18 x 16in)

Felt for hair and eyes: two pieces, each 23 x 30cm (9 x 12in)

Dresses fabric: two different fabrics, each 38 x 67.5cm (15 x 26½in)

For Little Lady's dress: two pieces of lace, 2.5cm (1in) wide by 11.5cm (4½in) long, and 10cm (4in) of scalloped edge lace

For Wild Flower's dress: two pieces of 4 x 11.5cm (4½ x 1½in) accent fabric or satin ribbon

Toy stuffing

Lining (optional), 25 x 67.5cm (10 x 26½in)

FABRIC COLOUR NOTES

I wanted the two different fabrics of the dresses to reflect the two different sides to Mia's personality. For Little Lady I chose a delicate rose print, cultivated and tidy, to show Mia's dressed up and smart side. For Wild Flower I chose a more rambling print with the essence of a wild garden or meadow, to reflect the free spirit side of Mia, running with her hair down through a meadow.

Cutting

- For all pattern piece templates, see Templates.
- Body: cut two 46cm (18in) squares from plain fabric.
- Skirts: cut 27 x 67.5cm (10½ x 26½in) from each of the dress fabrics.
- Dress top: cut two pattern pieces out of each of the dress fabrics.
- Hair: cut two back of head pattern pieces, cut one Little Lady hair front pattern piece and one bun pattern piece, cut one Wild Flower hair front pattern piece and four bunches pattern pieces.
- Eyes: cut four eye pattern pieces.

Tip

You will only need to use a lining to the skirts (see Stuffing the dolls and adding the skirts, step 3) if the fabric you have chosen for one or both of the dresses is very see-through or sheer.

All edge stitching and stitching close to the edge or fold is at 2mm (1/16in) from the edge unless otherwise stated.

Making

The dolls' bodies and dress tops

1 Make a copy of the doll body pattern (see Templates). Pin the pattern to the doll body fabric and draw around it. Unpin the pattern and flip it around, aligning the bottom of the pattern with the bottom of the drawn line, then pin and draw around again. Repeat with the other doll body fabric piece.

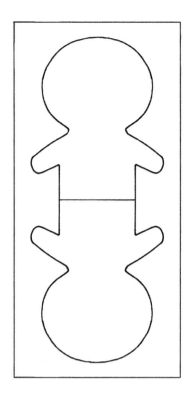

Don't cut the doll shape out.

2 Take one of your doll body pieces, turn it over and hold it up to a window so you can see the doll outline. Trace the doll body outline on to the other side, so you have the doll outline exactly aligned on both sides of the fabric. You will be using the line on this side to align the clothes, face and hair to. (You will use the line marked on the other side to follow later when you stitch the doll body pieces together, in step 1 of Stuffing the dolls and adding the skirts.)

3 Prepare the dress tops: fold over 5mm (¼in) to the wrong side at the cuffs of the sleeves and neckline of the four dress top pieces. Press.

4 Position Little Lady's dress top on one doll body (the top will overhang the doll outline by about 5mm (¼in) at the sleeves and sides). Stitch in place at the cuffs (close to the fold you made in step 3) and around the neck, following the curve of the folded neckline. Position Wild Flower's dress top at the opposite end of the doll and stitch in place also.

5 Repeat step 4 with the other doll body.

6 Align the 2.5cm (1in) wide lace with the bottom of Little Lady's dress top and stitch in place along both long edges of the lace. Repeat on the other doll body. Align the scalloped lace with the neckline and stitch in place along both long edges. This is now the front side of your doll.

7 Fold over 5mm (¼in) on one edge of both pieces of Wild Flower's accent fabric. Position and stitch in place as you did in step 6. Repeat on the back side of the doll.

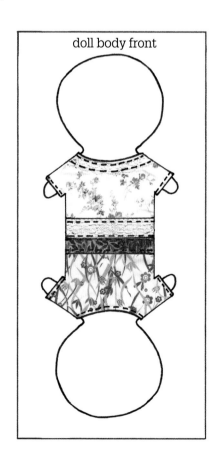

doll body front

The dolls' hair and faces

1. On the front of the doll, position Little Lady's front hair. The hair felt will overhang the doll outline by 5mm (¼in) around the sides of the head. Stitch along the fringe edge with co-ordinating thread, close to the edge. Sew a few stitches at the top of the head to hold the hair in place. Repeat with Wild Flower's hair at the opposite end of the doll.

2. Tape your face pattern piece (see Templates) to a window and hold your doll's front over it. Trace the eyes and mouth with a sharp pencil. Position the felt eyes on Little Lady, hold in place with a dab of washable glue and sew in place. Stitch the lashes and mouth. I used a sewing machine but you can hand sew using backstitch (see Hand sewing stitches in the Techniques section) if preferred. Repeat for Wild Flower.

Tip

Trim your threads close to the fabric, so that the thread ends don't show through on the right side of the face.

3. On the back side of the doll, place the back of the head hair on Little Lady's head, with a 5mm (¼in) overhang around the sides and top of the head. Stitch close to the edge at the nape of the neck. Sew a few stitches at the top of the head. Repeat at the opposite end of the doll for Wild Flower.

4. For Little Lady's bun, sew a gather stitch (a long running stitch, see Hand sewing stitches) 5mm (¼in) from the edge of the bun fabric piece, leaving long threads. Pull the thread ends up to gather the bun and knot them together. Stuff a small piece of toy stuffing into the bun and tuck the edges inside. Stitch in place on the back of Little Lady's head.

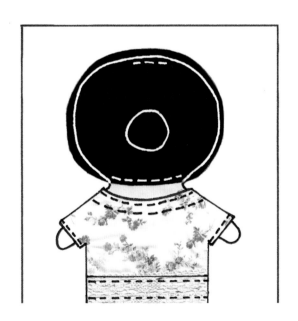

5 For Wild Flower's pigtails, stack two of the bunches fabric pieces and stitch them together, using co-ordinating thread, close to the edge. Repeat to make a second pigtail with the other two bunches pieces.

6 Position the pigtails at the base of the back of Wild Flower's head, as shown in the diagram below. Stitch them in place close to the edge of the head, with the tips of the pigtails flipped in towards the centre of the head.

Stuffing the dolls and adding the skirts

1 Place the front and back of the dolls' body right sides together, and align them carefully. Pin them together and stitch along the outline that you drew in Making, step 2. Leave a 5cm (2in) gap at one side. Be sure to backstitch (see Hand sewing stitches in the Techniques section) to secure your stitches at the beginning and end. Cut out around the doll outline to leave a seam allowance of 5mm (¼in). Clip the curves. Turn the dolls' body right side out through the gap.

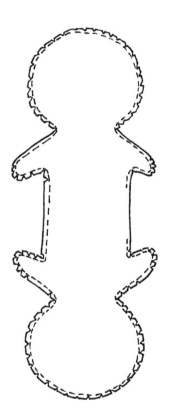

2 Stuff the dolls using small clumps of stuffing. Push the stuffing into the arms using the end of a pencil. Keep adding more clumps, creating the shape as you go. This process takes longer and more stuffing than you might expect! You are aiming for a firm feel. Slip stitch the gap closed (see Hand sewing stitches in the Techniques section).

3 Next prepare Little Lady's skirt. If you are using a lining, align this with the wrong side of your dress fabric. This will now be treated as one skirt piece.

4 Finish the top edge of the skirt with zigzag stitch (see Finishing the seam in Techniques).

5 With right sides together, form a skirt loop, stitching the edges together with a 1cm (⅜in) seam. Finish the seam (see Techniques) and press to one side. This is the back seam of the skirt.

6 Hem the bottom edge of the skirt by folding up 1.25cm (½in) and pressing. Fold another 2.5cm (1in) over, and press again. Stitch all around the hem, close to the fold.

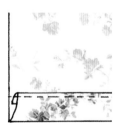

7 Next gather the top edge of the skirt. Starting at the back seam, 5mm (¼in) from the top finished edge, tack (baste) gathering stitches by hand or by adjusting your sewing machine stitch length to 4.5 or 5, all around the top edge of skirt.

Tip

When making your gathering stitches, leave long threads at the beginning and end of the stitching. When you've pulled your gathers to the desired length, tie the long threads together.

8 Pull the skirt over Little Lady's head, right sides together. Pull up the gathering stitches until the skirt fits the doll snugly. Ease the gathers along the stitches until they are even. Tie the threads together. Align the top finished edge of the skirt with the bottom of the lace (at the middle of the doll) and stitch in place along your gathering stitches. Using a thimble will make this more comfortable to do.

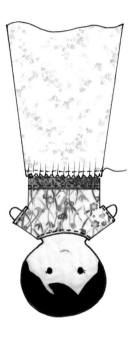

9 Repeat steps 3 to 8 with Wild Flower's skirt.

10 Slip stitch or ladder stitch (see Hand sewing stitches in the Techniques section) the bottom edges of the skirts together. Now go out and play!

Mia Doll

Poppy Accessories

These gorgeous, collectible accessories make adorable little presents, party bag fillers or projects to make together.

Friendship bracelets are a great way of using up scraps – you can either make a simple plain band or a textured plait, and even add a charm if you fancy. Super-pretty scrunchies can be worn on her wrist or in her hair, and won't pull it either. These are great for brightening up a little girl's outfit. Finally, rosettes are a wonderful birthday gift, adaptable to any special event you want to celebrate together.

Go forth and accessorize!

Hair scrunchie
You will need

Fabric, 10cm (4in) wide by 55cm (22in) or 65cm (26in) long (see Tip)

Elastic, 5mm (¼in) wide, 25cm (10in) long

FABRIC COLOUR NOTES

I chose coral colours for the scrunchies, but these look fab in any colour! I kept the print size of the flowers small. For the rosette, pick your recipient's favourite colour for a personalized touch.

Tip

The fabric you need for this scrunchie can be made by cutting a 10cm (4in) strip off any fat quarter of fabric that measures 55cm (22in) long for regular fabric and 65cm (26in) long for Liberty fabric.

Making

1 Fold your fabric strip in half lengthways, with right sides together. Stitch along the long edge with a 5mm (¼in) seam to make a tube.

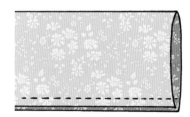

2 Turn the fabric tube right side out (see Techniques section).

3 Fasten a safety pin to one end of the elastic then push it into your fabric tube. Fasten the other end of the elastic to the same end of the fabric tube (so you don't lose this end inside). Feed the elastic through the tube using your forefingers and thumbs.

4 Pull both ends of the elastic clear of the fabric tube, tighten to the desired length and tie in an overhand knot, leaving elastic 'tails' about 2.5cm (1in) long. Trim the tails.

5 Fold in 1.25cm (½in) at one end of your tube.

6 Push the raw end of the tube into the folded end and slip stitch closed, hiding the elastic inside..

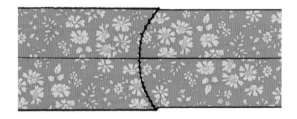

Bracelets

You will need

For a plain bracelet

Fabric, 4 x 30cm (1½ x 12in)

A charm on a jump ring or loop (optional)

For a plaited bracelet

Fabric, three strips each 4 x 30cm (1½ x 12in)

A charm on a jump ring or loop (optional)

Making

For a plain bracelet

1 Take your fabric strip and fold it in half along the length, right sides together. Sew with a 5mm (¼in) seam along the long edge to make a fabric tube. Turn the fabric tube right side out (see Techniques section).

2 If you are adding a charm to the bracelet, thread it on to the fabric strip. Knot the ends together with an overhand knot to fit the wrist.

For a plaited bracelet

1 Take one of your fabric strips and fold it in half along the length, right sides together. Sew with a 5mm (¼in) seam along the long edge to make a fabric tube. Turn the fabric tube right side out (see Techniques section). Repeat with the remaining two strips.

2 Plait the three fabric ribbons together, adding a charm halfway along if you wish, and knot the ends together with an overhand knot to fit the wrist.

Rosette

You will need

Fabric, 5 x 43cm (2 x 17in)

Felt, 7.5 x 13cm (3 x 5in)

Ribbons, 30cm (12in) each of three different ribbons

One brooch back pin

Cutting

- Felt: cut one circle for the rosette backing using the circle template (see Templates); cut a number, letter or star to decorate the front of the rosette (you choose!).

Tip

Make the central motif on your rosette fit the occasion you want to celebrate! Draw or print out the shape, or choose a letter in a font you like. I used Arial Rounded MT Bold, size 00.

Making

1 Fold a ribbon in half lengthways and snip at an angle across one end to give a 'V' shaped notch at the end of the ribbon, this will stop the ribbon from fraying. Repeat the cut at other end of the ribbon. Repeat for the other two ribbons.

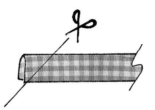

2 Align the ribbons and fold in half, then slightly spread the ribbons apart and sew onto the felt circle about 1.25cm (½in) from the bottom edge.

3 Sew a row of long tacking (basting) stitches along the bottom edge of the fabric strip (see Hand sewing stitches in Techniques section), leaving long threads. Pull up the thread ends to gather and spread the outer edge of the fabric around into a circle. Fold one end of the strip, wrong side together, and overlap on top of the other end of the strip (see diagram). This is the front of the rosette. Cut your letter, number or motif out of felt, glue in place on the front of the rosette and stitch close to the edge all around.

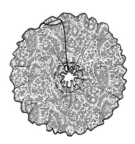

4 Pin the rosette front onto the felt circle so the ribbons are sandwiched in between. Machine zigzag stitch (see Techniques) in a circle or triangle to secure the inner edge of ruffled strip, ensuring the ends of the strip are tucked behind the felt.

5 Hand sew the brooch back onto the felt on the back of the rosette.

Techniques

Here is some advice together with some instructions that I hope will help you to complete and care for the lovely things that you have made.

Washing

When using Liberty fabrics I don't pre-wash as it is such a high quality fabric that shrinkage is negligible. For all other fabrics I would recommend pre-washing to check colourfastness. Colours will last longer if washed at a lower temperature with *no* laundry bleach. If you are mixing and matching types of fabrics, especially vintage with new, check that they can all be washed at the same temperature.

I like to make practical, usable items so all of the projects in this book are machine washable, except the lampshade, baskets and the doll (depending on what toy stuffing you use). For the Hannah t-shirt dress, pre-wash the t-shirt (perhaps with a scrap of white fabric in the wash) to check that the colour won't bleed into the lovely skirt you are about to add. For the Fleur embellished skirt, check the ribbons are washable in the same way.

You may wish to pre-wash wadding (batting) before quilting. Without pre-washing, once the whole quilt is made and washed it will take on a more puckered or 'quilt-y' look.

Cutting

Be mindful when cutting out patterns to keep the wastage to a minimum: position and cut out a pattern near the edge of the fabric. 'Fussy' cutting is where you position a particular part of the pattern, for example a whole flower, in the centre of whatever pattern piece or square of fabric you are cutting. This way of cutting usually causes more waste but if you keep all the scraps it's not such a problem.

Rotary cutting is a great way to accurately cut large quantities of fabric, such as the amount you would need for a quilt. But you will need a special rotary cutter, a grid ruler and a self-heal cutting mat to do it. These are not essential for the projects in this book, but if you are interested you could visit your local fabric store, look online or check out any good book on quilt making for advice.

Pinning

If you position your pins at right angles to the edge of the fabric you can sew straight over the pins (my preference) or, if you prefer, you can easily pull them out as the sewing machine needle approaches.

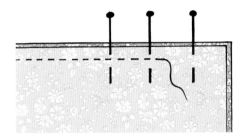

Seams

The seam allowance

This is the distance from the cut edge of the fabric to the line of stitching. Sewing accurate seams is the key to successful sewing. It may take some practise and there are various options for helping you to sew at the desired seam allowance:

❀ You can align the edge of the fabric with the markings on the throat plate (underneath the presser foot) of your sewing machine, if it has them.

❀ If your sewing machine doesn't have markings, measure the distance from the needle to the seam allowance and place a strip of masking tape on the throat plate as a guide.

❀ Some sewing machines allow adjustment of needle position so you can set this to the correct seam allowance and align the edge of the presser foot with the edge of the fabric.

❀ All the quilting is done with a ¼in seam allowance, so you may wish to use a ¼in presser foot. This is the equivalent to about 5mm, but the vast majority of quilting is done in inches, hence the seam allowance is given as ¼in.

Finishing a seam

If you see the instruction 'finish the seam' this simply means that you need to finish off the raw edges of the fabric with zigzag stitch and it is easy to do this using your sewing machine. Follow the handbook to see how to set your machine for zigzag stitch then, as you stitch, aim to have one side of the zigzag stitch through the fabric and the other side to be just off the edge. This will enclose the raw edges with stitching and prevent fraying.

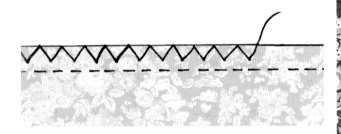

Chain piecing

This is a speedy method for sewing patchwork squares together. For example, for step 1 of the Sophie quilt: stitch one set of squares together along the seam allowance to create the desired unit, but don't cut the threads; leave the presser foot down and feed in another set of squares, stitching across the gap and along this set of squares. Feed in another set of squares, keep stitching, and repeat. When you have sewn all the sets of squares, snip the threads between the units to separate them.

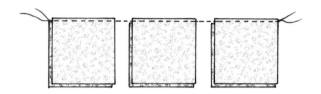

Turning fabric tubes right side out

Here's a clever way to turn long thin tubes of fabric, such as bag straps, the right way out. You will need to use this method for the tabs on the Natasha tab top curtains, the handles of the Isabel baskets, the fabric ribbons that make the strap on the Molly purse, the drawstring for the Sara drawstring bag and the Poppy accessories bracelets.

1 Attach safety pins to both ends of a 65cm (25in) long piece of string and pin one safety pin to one side of your tube.

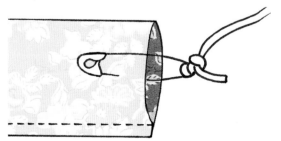

2 Post the other safety pin down the tube and, using your thumb and forefinger, push and slide it along inside the tube to the other end.

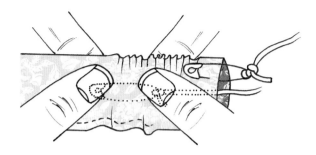

3 Pull the posted safety pin out and pull the other end with the safety pin attached through the tube.

Hand sewing stitches
Ladder stitch

Useful for closing gaps to finish projects that need to be turned inside out during the making. Stitch as shown and pull up to close the gap.

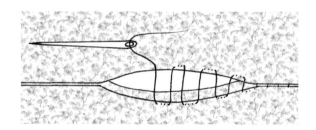

Slip stitch

Another good gap-closing stitch and very simple to do, just stitch as shown and pull up to close the gap.

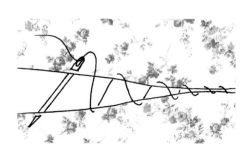

Running stitch

The simplest stitch of all, running stitch is often used for tacking (basting) and gathering.

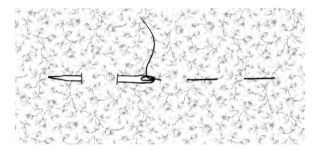

Backstitch

This is a straight stitch going in the opposite direction to the last stitch you made. A few backstitches can be used to secure the beginning and end of a line of stitching.

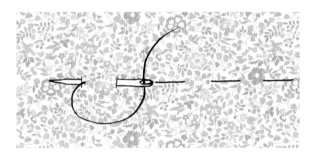

Blanket stitch

A great stitch for finishing the edges of appliquéd motifs, try it in co-ordinating or contrasting thread.

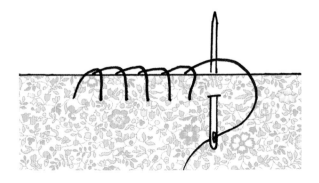

Making buttonholes

1 Measure your button and draw a line this length on your fabric where you want the buttonhole to be. Referring to your sewing machine manual, set the zigzag stitch to a long length and width setting, to sew a bar tack across the top of the line.

2 Readjust the zigzag stitch to a short length and width setting, and stitch a line of tight, narrow zigzag stitches down one side of the line.

3 Sew another bar tack at the bottom of the line, and repeat step 2 along the other side of the line.

4 Cut along the marked line with a seam ripper, taking care not to cut through any stitches.

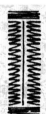

Templates

Mia Doll
Use the templates at actual size

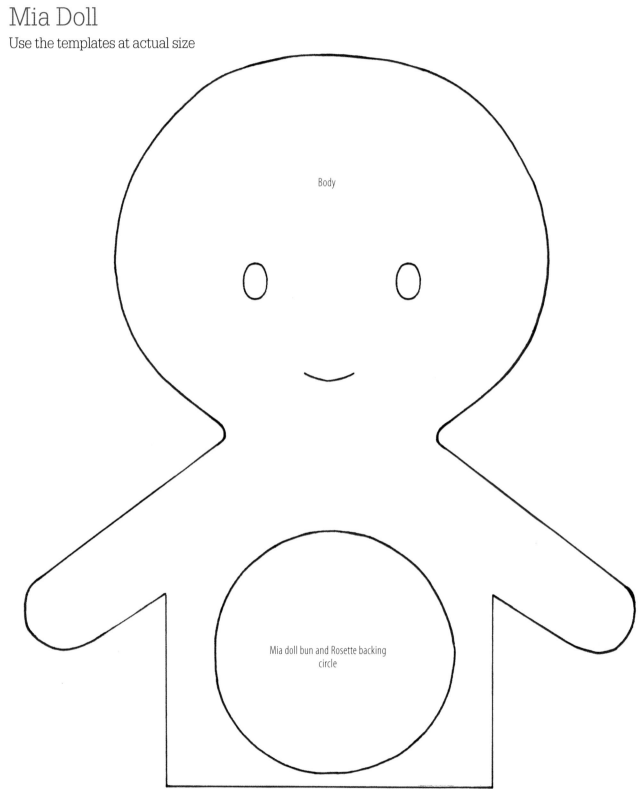

Body

Mia doll bun and Rosette backing circle

Wild Flower hair front

Wild Flower bunches

Little Lady hair front

Dress top

Natasha Tab Top Curtains
Enlarge butterflies by 200%

Molly Purse
Enlarge by 200%

About the Author

Alice has always loved playing with fabrics, finding particular joy in combining colours. Finding a snippet of Liberty amongst her grandmother's quilting stash of worn out dresses and vintage fabrics was always a highlight and from there her passion for Liberty fabrics grew. Trained in scientific research, she kept her passion for sewing alive throughout her Ph.D in genetics, selling handmade bags at student fairs. It is from here that she started her business, Alice Caroline. Alice now enjoys running her business and designing sewing patterns and kits, which are stocked in the iconic Liberty of London store. Alice Caroline specializes in Liberty fabrics, sending Liberty fabrics, patterns and kits all over the world.

Alice lives and works in Gloucestershire, UK.

Acknowledgments

This book is dedicated to all grandmothers who pass on sewing skills, encouraging creativity and a love of sewing in future generations.

Thank you so much to Ame for all your work in making this book happen, for liking what I do with fabric and asking if I'd like to write a book about it. Thank you to Charly for bringing it all together beautifully, Emma for co-ordinating everything and to Cheryl for your diligent editorial work. Thank you to Jane also. Thank you to Jack for your fabulous photography. Thank you to Katherine, wordsmith, I am awed by your way with words and am grateful for your willing contribution to this book. Will, for all your support and patience. Sophie and Lawrence lights of my life. Mum for teaching me to sew and inspiring a lifetime love of colour. My sister Helen for being awesome. To everyone at Alice Caroline: Anna, Caroline, Hils, Pauline, Sara and Sarah for all of your skills, dedication and fun.

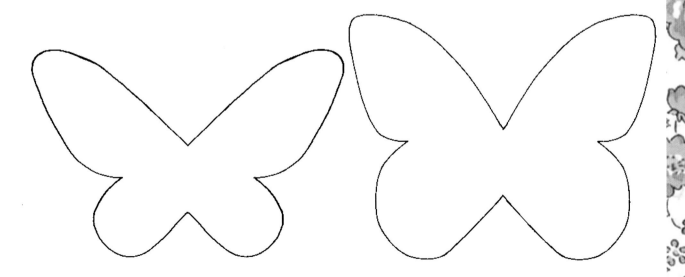

Suppliers List

Fabrics

Stitch Craft Create
www.stitchcraftcreate.co.uk

Etsy
www.etsy.com
An awesome resource for all fabric and crafting supplies, as well as handmade items.

Oakshott
www.oakshott.com
Beautiful plain and shot cottons.

Liberty stockists

UK

Liberty
www.Liberty.co.uk
Wonderful department store, Regent Street, London.

Alice Caroline
www.alicecaroline.co.uk
Specialist Liberty fabric stockist, with an ever growing selection of seasonal and classic prints. Worldwide shipping.

AUSTRALIA

Materialise Your Life
www.materialiseyourlife.com
Patchwork store, 2 / 51 Aberdare Road, Nedlands, Western Australia 6009.

USA

Purl Soho
www.purlsoho.com
Beautiful rainbow filled store, 459 Broome Street, New York, NY 10013.
Also their blog is brimming with inspirational craft projects: www.purlbee.com

JAPAN

Lilymeru
www.lilymeru.etsy.com
Liberty Japan & Hello Kitty X Liberty fabrics!

Tokyu Hands
Crafting super-stores, at various locations throughout Japan. My dream shop!

Haberdashery and sundries

Ernest Wright
www.ernestwright.co.uk
An amazing range of scissors for all sorts of uses, still hand forged in Sheffield, UK, using traditional methods.

Zipit
www.zipit.etsy.com
An awesome selection of YKK zips in many colours and lengths. Worldwide shipping.

The Cotton Patch
www.cottonpatch.co.uk
A wide range of wadding (batting) and quilting supplies.

VV Rouleaux
www.vvrouleaux.com
Ribbons galore! Wonderful shop at 102 Marylebone Lane, London W1U 2QD.

Index

A DAVID & CHARLES BOOK
© F&W Media International, Ltd 2015

David & Charles is an imprint of F&W Media International, Ltd
Brunel House, Forde Close, Newton Abbot, TQ12 4PU, UK

F&W Media International, Ltd is a subsidiary of F+W Media, Inc
10151 Carver Road, Suite #200, Blue Ash, OH 45242, USA

ISBN-13: 978-1-4463-0495-2 paperback UK edition
ISBN-10: 1-4463-0495-7 paperback UK edition

ISBN-13: 978-1-4463-0496-9 paperback US edition
ISBN-10: 1-4463-0496-5 paperback US edition

ISBN-13: 978-1-4463-6913-5 PDF UK edition
ISBN-10: 1-4463-6913-7 PDF UK edition

ISBN-13: 978-1-4463-6915-9 PDF US edition
ISBN-10: 1-4463-6915-3 PDF US edition

ISBN-13: 978-1-4463-6912-8 EPUB UK edition
ISBN-10: 1-4463-6912-9 EPUB UK edition

ISBN-13: 978-1-4463-6914-2 EPUB US edition
ISBN-10: 1-4463-6914-5 EPUB US edition

Printed in China by RR Donnelley for:
F&W Media International, Ltd
Brunel House, Forde Close, Newton Abbot, TQ12 4PU, UK

10 9 8 7 6 5 4 3 2 1

Content Director: Ame Verso
Editor: Emma Gardner
Project Editors: Jane Trollope and Cheryl Brown
Art Editor: Charly Bailey
Photographer: Jack Kirby
Production Manager: Beverley Richardson

F+W Media publishes high quality books on a wide range of subjects.
For more great book ideas visit: www.stitchcraftcreate.co.uk

Layout of the digital edition of this book may vary depending on reader hardware and display settings.